# *Jessica on*

by the same author

*

THE BUS GIRLS
SERAPHINA
EMILY AND THE HEADMISTRESS

MARY K. HARRIS

# *Jessica on Her Own*

*illustrated by*

ALISON PRINCE

FABER FANFARES

*First published in 1968*
*by Faber and Faber Limited*
*3 Queen Square London WC1*
*First published in Fanfares edition 1978*
*Printed in Great Britain by*
*Jarrold & Sons Ltd, Norwich*



*British Library Cataloguing in Publication Data*
*Harris, Mary Kathleen*
*Jessica on her own. – (Faber fanfares).*
*I. Title*
*823'.9'1J PZ7.H24Z3*

*ISBN 0–571–11276–5*

# *Contents*

## *Contents*



## *Acknowledgement*


Permission for the use of an extract from "Sea Fever" by John Masefield on p. 7 has been given by the Society of Authors as the literary representatives of the Estate of John Masefield.

# I

# *The Policeman*

Until Isabel came there had been just the three of them: Rosalind, Jessica and Sophie. Sophie was only eight years old, and she still attended the Miss Fanshawes' preparatory school called "The Limes"; Rosalind, the eldest, went to Westbridge Grammar School; and Jessica went reluctantly to the Secondary Modern.

Jessica would have gone reluctantly to school anywhere. She liked to lie in bed in the mornings until the last possible moment planning her home for stray cats, or repeating to herself such nice things as:

"*I must go down to the seas again, to the lonely sea and the sky. . . .*"

On this particular morning—which was the beginning of the hot summer, the beginning of everything—Jessica could hear her small sister panting zealously as she stripped her bed and then folded and patted her pyjamas into a neat square. "Sophie is so perfect, she cannot be long for this world," thought Jessica, luxuriating in her own sinful nature as she snuggled down.

"Jess, is that you I don't hear getting up yet?"

That was her mother calling up the stairs, in what Jessica called her "amused" voice. So no need to stir yet. . . . Twelve cats with twelve saucers of porridge.

"Jessica! If you're not down in five minutes. . . ."

There was nothing for it. Jessica tumbled out of bed, splashed cold water over her face, flung on her clothes, and came cautiously downstairs.

Her mother was in the hall phoning an agitated helper about the door-to-door collection for the Freedom from Hunger Campaign. She was speaking in her half-laughing, reassuring, leave-it-all-to-me voice, but she managed to combine this with a cool surprised stare at her daughter's head as Jessica slithered guiltily past.

The dining-room was fresh with early-morning sunlight and smelt of coffee and toast. Mr. Rendell, hidden behind *The Telegraph*, took no notice when Jessica burst in, but Sophie and Rosalind stared: Sophie, silent and unfriendly over the rim of her mug, Rosalind, all sparkling vitality.

"Gosh! you look a sketch this morning."

"What's the matter? I've washed."

"Your hair, my dear."

Jessica passed a hand over the top of her head. She had forgotten to do it. Dismissing the discovery, she picked up her spoon and drew it through the island of porridge, making it wobble in its sea of milk.

"It's quite cold!"

Mr. Rendell lowered his newspaper. "You won't want porridge at all in a day or two. There's a heat wave on the way. They're frying eggs on the pavement in New York."

DAILY

"Oh, how delicious!" Jessica cried.

"You revolting child," said Rosalind. "Where everybody's walked, including dogs!"

"I'd scrub the pavement first."

"I'd like to see you."

Their father folded his paper and rose from the table. He flipped Jessica lightly on the head as he went by her chair, and Jessica ducked and grinned. A rude little girl had once said to her, "Your father is just like a monkey," and certainly he wasn't all that handsome. But who cared, when he'd got such kind eyes and such a nice, warm smile?

"Ready, Tiddles?" he said to Sophie.

Sophie got up at once. Mr. Rendell drove her every morning as far as the hospital where he worked, which was in the same road as "The Limes".

Rosalind had also left the breakfast table. She came in again with her straw boater and was now setting it on her head in front of the dining-room looking-glass. She was one of those lucky people who can look at themselves with satisfaction. She did so now. The hard straw made her look prettier than ever, golden and glowing.

"I wish we had hats like that," said Jessica. "My beret is always getting trodden in the dust by clod-hoppers."

"You should have worked harder and got into the Grammar School," said Rosalind, in her easy way. "We haven't any boys to trample on our hats there."

Jessica pulled a face. It was extraordinary how everything seemed to come round to the fact that when she took the 11 plus, she had been found wanting; even now, two years after the blow had fallen. But Rosalind's casual remarks were easier to shake off than her mother's determination that Jessica should not get "left behind". She had convinced the Secondary Modern Head that Jessica must be put in the "A"-stream, where they worked them hard from the start and held out the lure of O-levels and C.S.E.'s. What her mother could not grasp was that all her kindness and tact was wasted: Jessica simply had no love of books, and that was that.

She heard the car door bang. Through the open window she could see her father backing his car on to the road with Sophie seated beside him like royalty. She was holding a bunch of roses for her dear Miss Fanshawe. "She's an odd fish," thought Jessica. "There are only two people in the world for her, besides herself—Mum and Miss F."

Left to herself, Jessica flung herself on the floor with the remains of her toast and a comic. Alas, she was not allowed long to remain in peace. Mrs. Rendell looked in with one of her semi-humorous questions.

"I wonder how much longer I have got to wait for the breakfast things?"

Jessica scrambled up guiltily.

"Oh, Jess, not a comic! And you a big girl of twelve. Even Sophie doesn't read them now."

Jessica shut her mouth tight. Sophie did read comics, but only when nobody was looking. . . .

"Well, clear the table for me, like a kind girl," said her mother. "That's all I ask you to do."

I lead a dog's life, thought Jessica. She began to pile the china higgledy-piggledy on to the tray.

"Darling, *not* like that. What is the matter with you this morning?"

"I feel *exactly* the same as I always do."

"You'll look better when you've given your hair a good brush. Upstairs with you quickly, or you'll be late."

Jessica banged her hair with a brush. She couldn't admire it. Sophie's was dark and silky like a Chinese, Rosalind's hair was a golden aureole. *Her* hair was straw-coloured. She combed her fringe and practised her dark, suspicious glance at the same time.

The sun made the morning warm already. Jessica dawdled along to school, enjoying the heat, and thinking how nice it would be if her mother went out to work. She imagined herself as a latch-key kid, returning every afternoon to an empty house, raiding the larder and casting herself down with a chunk of cake and a comic before everyone else came in to spoil things. The trouble with her mother was that she *knew* too much. She was an M.A. Cantab. and had taught Geography before she married. Why couldn't she go back to teaching? At Rosalind's school, of course, not hers.

At this point in her day-dream Jessica found herself at the edge of the curb. She stopped and waited to cross over. Cars came swooshing round the corner almost non-stop round about nine o'clock. They roared their way up the new wide road, past the crumbling wall of the Manor on one side and the new housing estate branching off on the other, up the rise to the huge engineering works at the top. Bored, Jessica gazed idly back the way she had come.

A policeman was just turning in at the gate of her house.

Jessica could see quite clearly that it was her house because it stood almost facing her on the curve of the crescent. She could see the wrought-iron gate and the path edged with standard roses leading to the front door.

A policeman. . . . He had knocked; the door had been opened; he had disappeared inside. What did he want? Had she done anything? Numerous peccadillos rose in Jessica's mind but, thank goodness, nothing really bad . . . Then . . . then had something awful happened to one of her family, something too awful and too adult for her to know anything about? Had her father damaged a patient by mistake? He was always telling funny stories of patients who came back saying his massage had made them feel much worse . . .

Suddenly she woke to the fact that she was still waiting on the curb. She thought she saw a gap in the traffic, ducked her head and plunged blindly across. Brakes screeched and a car came to a dead halt a foot from her nose. For a second the whole world seemed to halt too. Then a red face glared at her from the car window.

"Can't you look where you're going?"

With shaking legs Jessica scuttled to the opposite pavement.

She had only taken a few steps when a voice hailed her.

"Hi, kid! Wait for us!"

It was her friend, Nance Parker, all long legs and bumping satchel as she ran to overtake her. Nance lived in one of the council houses off the new road and was a girl of strange ideas. One of them was that she hadn't been offered a place in the Grammar School because her father was a dustman. There was no doubt about it, Nance exercised her brains. Her hand shot up in class on every possible occasion; and not only to answer questions, but to ask them. Most of them boiled down to "Why don't somebody *do* something about it?" or "It's not right, that's what I say." For Nance was a rebel, a regular soap-box orator, a champion of the under-dog. Sometimes Jessica had the impression that Nance regarded *her* as a sort of under-dog.

"My, that was nearly the finish of you," observed Nance, panting at her side.

Jessica grinned weakly.

"If you'd been killed, I wonder what the Head would have said about you? When Cassy Mallow in Primary died, we sang:

> "*Around the throne of God a band*
> *Of glorious angels ever stand*"

as if Cassy was one of 'em. Kid, I just can't see you as a glorious angel."

Jessica hastily changed the subject.

"Nance, if a policeman was to call at your house, what would you suppose he'd come for?"

"Call at our house? They'd better not try!" Nance bristled up at once. "You should hear what my Dad has to say about some of those cubs dressed up in uniform!"

"Nance, I don't really mean your house. I mean mine."

"Yours? Honest? When?"

"Just now. Just before I nearly got . . ."

"Crikey! You in trouble with the police!" Nance was tall, and she glanced down her long, thin nose at Jessica as if she were years younger than herself and needed protecting. "Well, I don't know: it might be an eviction order. If you haven't coughed up the rent . . ."

"We don't pay rent."

"No, of course, it couldn't be that, could it? You're posh."

"We're not posh!" Jessica hated Nance when she stressed this gulf between them.

"All right, all right. Now, let me think. . . . A policeman called on our Mrs. Bone when her old man was knocked down in the street."

"Oh no, no—it *couldn't* be that!"

"Look, kid, it's no good you saying 'couldn't' to everything."

Jessica's face worked. She had a wild urge to rush back home and burst into her house, crying, "Is everyone safe?"

Nance's sharp, kind eyes missed nothing. She had been treating the question as she treated all questions, as interesting topics for speculation, worthy of all her intellectual resources. But Jess was looking proper upset.

"Huh, don't you start worrying now. I bet it was just some old bobby hawking tickets for the Police Jumble Sale."

But Jessica's recent experience in crossing the road had made an accident into a frightening possibility. Suppose it was Sophie? She did have one crossing to make on her own after Daddy had dropped her at the hospital. Oh, not Sophie. . . . Yet hadn't she, herself, that very morning, thought in a jeering sort of way, "Sophie is so good, she cannot be long for this world"? Had God snatched the words from her lips, made them true? Please, not

Sophie. . . . Mum would never, never get over it. Sophie was her darling, her treasure, her joy. . . . Oh, if only I hadn't been so awful this morning. . . . It was a moment of light for Jessica. Suddenly she saw herself as she was, cussed, lazy and . . . and something much worse. Why, she'd actually wished that her mother was less at home, as if her mother . . . Sophie . . . the whole family, meant nothing to her at all. . . .

"Jess . . ." Nance had actually grasped her arm in order to attract her attention—"don't look like that. I wish I hadn't said anything."

"So do I!"

"Honest, Jess, they do come round hawking their tickets for Sports Day."

"You always do have the most *awful* ideas . . ."

But it was not a good moment in which to take umbrage at Nance. They had arrived at the school gates and were part of a turbulent stream of boys and girls. Already Jessica had drawn closer to her friend. Boys . . . Jessica hated them; not the boys in her own class, they weren't too bad, but the bigger boys. They wheeled their bicycles close on her hurrying heels, played football with her beret, shoved spiders down her back. Boys were awful. Jessica could not understand anybody wanting a boy-friend.

But with Nance as her bodyguard even Syd Bulsher left her alone.

## 2

# *The Reason*

Mr. Berryman, Jessica's form-master, had once said to her: "Jessica, I always see you occupied in one of two things: either talking to your next-door neighbour or sleeping."

Jessica certainly found school very soporific. The familiar, stuffy smell of the class-room, the boredom of most of the lessons, the weight of passive indifference in at least half the class, all had a lethargic effect on her brains. Today was no exception; and although she had arrived at school worried to death, by the end of the afternoon she was dreaming in her desk in the back row and had almost forgotten that she had anything to worry about.

Nance was down for a swimming practice after school. She vanished, waving her scarlet swim-suit, and Jessica had to walk home alone. It was then that she left off being Jessica of 11A and returned to being Jessica with a home life and a load of apprehension. As the crescent came in sight she began to walk faster. Yet the morning's urge to rush in on her mother, crying, "Is everyone safe?" was now tempered by the consideration of what a goose she would look if everyone *was* safe. No, she must sense the atmosphere first. If anything awful had happened she would know fast enough.

The side-door was always left unlocked for her at this time of day. Jessica tiptoed into the kitchen as wary as a Sioux. Her mother, with her tall, familiar figure and knot of fair hair, was standing with her back to her at the stove, making the tea.

She exclaimed: "Oh, Jess, *don't* make me jump like that!" in exasperated, almost despairing tones; and then added: "Hurry up and wash your hands. Tea's ready."

Had anything happened . . . or hadn't it? Jessica walked slowly upstairs, and saw, through the open bathroom door, Sophie drying her hands on a towel.

So *she* was all right.

Completely all right by the look of her, and full of silent importance. You could see that she was all primed to tell Mum that she was the only one in the class to spell "Mediterranean" correctly.

Jessica made short work of her wash and came running downstairs again close on Sophie's heels. Their mother was at the tea-table. Sophie took her place, spread her napkin neatly on her knee, gave a wriggle, and said:

"Mummy, have you guessed?"

"Guessed . . .? No, darling."

Sophie gave her mother quite a severe look.

"Have you *tried* to guess?"

"Darling, suppose you tell me right away, and put me out of my . . ."

Had Mother been about to say "misery" and then shied away from the word?

"All right, I'll tell you, Mummy: I've been chosen out of every single person in the school to recite "The Pied Piper" at the Garden Party. The others act the mime while I say it."

"Darling, how wonderful. I am pleased."

Jessica narrowed her eyes. Was there a note of almost desperate enthusiasm in her mother's voice?

"I could recite it to you after tea. I know it all."

"Yes, yes, darling, we'll see . . . some time later on."

There *was* something wrong. Sophie herself was looking puzzled.

"Mum . . . where's Ros?" asked Jessica.

"Rosalind . . ." Her mother had two fingers pressed to her forehead. ". . . Isn't this her afternoon for tennis?"

So Ros was alive too. . . .

"Mum, have you got a headache?"

"Well, yes, I have . . . just a bit."

"I'll fetch you the aspirin."

"No, darling, it's all right. But I think I'll leave you two to get on with your tea."

Jessica and Sophie, left alone, stared at each other. There was little sympathy between them, but in that instant they were united in fear and surmise. Suddenly Jessica found that she had got up and was walking towards the door. It was just as if a new, adult Jessica whom she must obey had taken over. She followed her mother into the kitchen, and said, in a small, very grave voice:

"Mum, is anything the matter?"

Mrs. Rendell was facing the window. She turned round, and said, "Oh, Jess . . . yes. Yes, there is."

Jessica stood still, frightened; yet oddly relieved that she hadn't made a goose of herself.

"Not to us, darling," continued her mother hastily. "I mean—" she held out her hand to Jessica who shyly grasped it—"it's your Aunt Rachel and Uncle Graham. Last night . . . in a bad car crash . . ."

It was at this instant that Rosalind burst in on them, hot and glowing.

"Mum, I'm just about boiled!" She flung down her satchel and tennis racket, and then must have felt the tension in the air. "Hullo, Jessica having a pi-jaw?"

"No, I'm not!" flashed Jessica, a child again.

Mrs. Rendell repeated the news to Rosalind, who turned sober at once.

"Are they . . . were they . . .?"

"Yes . . . instantly."

"And . . . Isabel?"

"Isabel wasn't with them. She was in bed at home."

"Poor Isabel." Rosalind, still puffing and glowing, showed concern. "What will she do? She's a kind of orphan now, isn't she? Will she come to us?"

A *kind* of orphan? She *was* an orphan now. Puzzled, Jessica looked from one speaker to the other.

"I don't know anything yet, dear," replied her mother. "At the moment she's with a school friend. Now, run and have your tea."

It took a great deal to damp Rosalind's spirits entirely, and unlike Jessica and Sophie she ate quite a large tea. But she did give all her mind to the disaster.

"How ghastly for poor old Mum. Now she'll have to trek all the way up to Edinburgh for the funeral *and* make plans for Isabel. I bet she comes to live with us." She paused and stared at Sophie. "Cheer up, Tiddles," she said kindly.

Sophie certainly looked very down in the mouth. But she asked no questions and whether she was upset simply because her mother might not be able to give her whole, fond attention to "The Pied Piper" it was hard to say.

Rosalind and Jessica were still working at their lessons when Mr. Rendell arrived home from the hospital. He and their mother had a low-voiced conversation in the hall, and although Rosalind and Jessica both raised their heads and tried to listen, they couldn't make out a word. Then Mr. Rendell made a long distance call over the phone. This time they could make out a little. Mother was going up to Edinburgh.

Altogether it was a silent, oppressive evening. It was the change in her mother's voice which Jessica noticed more than anything. The familiar amused tone with its slight drawl was now flat and dry as if all the life had gone out of it. Sophie must have minded too. She sat before her glass of milk and biscuits before bed-time just staring at them and then suddenly, quite suddenly, burst into tears. Her tears proved a help. By the time she had been petted and comforted and allowed to watch television, wearing her dressing-gown and enthroned on her mother's knee, everyone was feeling better.

Nothing was said about the trip up to Edinburgh until the following evening.

Rosalind took a very firm line.

"Now, Mum, we're perfectly capable of looking

after ourselves for three or four days. Sophie's always good, and Jessica will have to be good."

"As long as Sophie doesn't have any of her nightmares, and you and Jessica don't break out into arguments over everything . . ." Mrs. Rendell paused; nothing could be read into Jessica's round stare from under her fringe. "I've left plenty of food in the larder, and Mrs. Rudge has promised to come in every afternoon. She'll bring salad stuff and fruit with her, and clean through and leave everything ready for the evening meal. Jessica, you are the one I am most concerned about . . ."

Jessica's eyes grew increasingly enigmatic.

"Now, please, please, do what Rosalind says without arguing. And as you insist on being the last off to school and the first home, I must entrust you with the key. Come and let me tie it round your neck."

Jessica pulled in her chin in order to see the key dangling from its cord.

"Why, I'm a latch-key kid! . . ."

# 3

## *Liberty Hall*

Mrs. Rendell left the house at eight o'clock the next morning. And then, after Jessica had banged the front door behind her, the house was empty all day except for Mrs. Rudge and Claudius, the cat.

Jessica came tearing home. She burst upstairs into her bedroom and found Claudius fast asleep in a round on her eiderdown. The picture of Claudius observing her mother's exit with a suitcase, putting two and two together, and sneaking upstairs to forbidden territory made her puff her chest with pride. Nobody could say that darling Claudius hadn't got brains. Carefully preserving his round shape, she gathered him up in her arms and went downstairs and straight to the larder. It really was crammed with good things. She put half a jam tart into her mouth and then tipped all the cream from a gold-topped bottle of milk into Claudius's saucer. Once again he proved his brains by attacking the cream with guilty haste.

Jessica watched him lovingly. She was dreaming of twelve stray cats all enjoying the best of the Jersey milk

when she heard voices along the side-passage. When she opened to Rosalind and Sophie banging on the side-door (she had forgotten to unlock it ready for them) she had the tea-pot in one hand and looked busy.

"Ros," said Jessica, when the three of them were seated in amity round the tea-table, "do you think Mum will bring Isabel home with her?"

"Spect so. Mum would never allow her to go back into an orphanage."

"Back into an *orphanage?*"

"Oh, Jess, surely you knew. Isabel was adopted."

Jessica was dumbfounded. She shifted her gaze to Sophie, who looked back with her dark, unwinking stare.

"Mummy never told me!"

"Why should she? You're such a kid."

"So she's not really our cousin?"

"No."

"Is that why we never meet?"

"Of course not. It just is that they live so far away. We had a combined summer holiday once when you were only four. And we were going to have another combined one the year before last, only you went and got measles. You would."

Jessica's interest was far too deeply engaged for once to take exception to Rosalind's remark. She insisted again:

"So you think she will come to us?"

"I'm sure Uncle Graham's side of the family won't want her. He's only got two unmarried sisters, both with jobs. But Aunt Rachel was Mum's twin, and they were terribly fond of each other. I can't see Mum *not* having Isabel: she's always the one to take things on."

Jessica brooded on this. Absence suddenly made her mother vivid; not just familiarly, as her mother, but as a person. Tall, cool, with smooth fair hair and blue eyes always a little critical—until they glanced at Sophie. And it was true that, even if she wasn't plump, bustling, and cosy, she was always doing things for people—driving old Mrs. Shaw to her "Derby and Joan" every Tuesday, lecturing to Women's Institutes, collecting for the Freedom from Hunger Campaign. Yes, Mother would have Isabel.

But their father said that evening, when he came in late and tired:

"I don't know. But you can take it that your mother will try and arrange things for the very best."

Liberty Hall began to lose some of its novelty by the end of the second day. For one thing, Jessica decided Rosalind wasn't playing fair. She had brought Clare home to tea with her. That was normal enough: Clare had tea with them every Thursday, and after the meal she and Rosalind would spend a cosy two hours with their homework and pop records shut up in Rosalind's bedroom. But today Rosalind, having filled Jessica's and Sophie's cups with tea, had decamped upstairs immediately with her friend, the tea-pot and a large share of the cake.

Jessica shrugged and spread both butter and jam on her gingerbread. She was bored sitting opposite to the silent Sophie, and brought the meal to an abrupt end. Soon she had lost herself in drawing a picture-map of the products of South America. She worked with exquisite care, her tongue between her teeth. She hardly heard the front door bang; but she did glance up when Rosalind burst into the room with her pile of books.

"I suppose she's jealous!"

"Who's jealous?"

"Clare, you silly. She says she's sick of the very name of Isabel. And when I said, 'Don't worry, she may never come,' she said, 'Why talk about her then?' "

"I expect you do talk too much about her. You talk too much about everything."

"Well, don't you talk about Isabel to Nance? Oh, well, Nance isn't touchy like Clare. Anyhow, the silly chump has rushed off in a pet. Jess—" Rosalind came and looked over her sister's shoulder—"is that all the homework you've done so far?"

Jessica leaned back as if to consider how complete her map was. Arguing with mother was one thing, because her mother was firm and had the last word; arguing with Rosalind was quite another thing, because it went on and on. Everything did seem very exhausting somehow with Mother away. She was just opening her mouth to tell Rosalind that the din from her records had naturally slowed down progress when Mr. Rendell came in. He had no hospital clinic on Thursday afternoons but saw one or two private patients at his house instead. The last patient had just gone, and instead of staying on in his study-cum-treatment room as he usually did to write up his notes, he decided to be with his children. He kissed them all, praised Sophie's page of sums, and then sank down in his armchair with a book, and closed his eyes.

Rosalind glanced at her father; he appeared to be

asleep. Quickly snatching up one of Jessica's exercise books, she looked inside it.

"You've been on that map for a whole hour, and you haven't even started on your French yet!"

"Leave my things alone!" hissed back Jessica, keeping her voice low.

"Mum said I was to see you did your homework properly and didn't mess about drawing all the evening."

"What about you taking the tea-pot upstairs!"

Mr. Rendell opened his eyes and coughed irritably.

Jessica hunched her shoulders and waited for her father to close his eyes again. She could not bear to see the tired, patient look on his face intensify through any fault of hers. She waited until his breathing was even again. Then she picked up her green crayon and went on with her map.

It was nothing but a gesture of defiance. If Rosalind hadn't interfered, she *would* have started her French by now. She felt Rosalind's accusing stare on her, and concentrated on printing "Maize crops" very neatly. Rosalind's hand suddenly shot out and snatched at her map. Jessica seized it just in time. As each tugged in silent fury, the telephone rang.

Jessica was the first out of her chair, the first to reach it. But no sooner had she lifted the receiver than her father was at her elbow, calmly taking it from her.

"Yes, yes . . . Oh, hullo, Lydia . . ."

"Ros, it's mother," said Jessica, tiptoing back into the dining-room.

Hostilities were forgotten. Jessica put her hand on her sister's shoulder, as they both listened hard.

". . . Yes, we're fine. . . . Tomorrow? . . .; then back the next day. . . . Oh, well, I quite see that. . . . Oh, just one or two little tiffs. . . . Yes, dear, Sophie's all right. . . ."

One or two little tiffs. Jessica's cheek crimsoned. She looked up, round-eyed, as her father returned to the dining-room.

"Mother sends you all her love. The funeral is to-morrow, and she hopes to be back on Saturday."

"Another whole day without her?" said Jessica, in disappointed tones.

"Will she bring Isabel with her?" asked Rosalind.

"I don't think so. Nothing has been decided yet. Your mother is going to have a talk with her head-mistress tomorrow. . . ."

Sophie had one of her nightmares that night and woke, screaming for her mother. Jessica, wakened by the screams, nipped out of bed and put the light on. Sophie was sitting up in bed, her eyes tight shut; Jessica could do nothing with her. Then Father came in, and Rosalind. "She's been so good up till now," said Rosalind, very motherly. Mr. Rendell lifted Sophie up into his arms and carried her off to share Rosalind's bed for the rest of the night. The excitement subsided. Jessica composed herself with a loud sigh. The broken night made her mother's absence seem interminable.

Mrs. Rendell travelled down from Edinburgh the following night and arrived home after breakfast on Saturday morning. She bundled Claudius out of the arm-chair and sat there herself with her arm round Sophie.

No, she hadn't brought Isabel back with her. Isabel was all right for the time being with her friend, Maimie.

Yes, Isabel was coming to live with them, on condition that she could get a transfer from her Edinburgh school to the Grammar School here.

It was Rosalind who had asked all the questions, her arms on the back of a chair, chin thrust forward.

"Oh, she must come to us! She's just the same age as me. It will be such fun if we're in the same form."

Mother stroked Sophie's fine, dark hair. She said: "Maimie's mother said that Isabel has always been in the "A" stream. But, of course, I knew that from Aunt Rachel. She was always telling me how good Isabel is at Geography."

"That will please you, Mum," said Rosalind shrewdly. And then added warmly: "Oh, I do hope she comes. She will be like a twin sister for me. Jess is such a baby."

Jessica hauled up Claudius into her arms. Mother hadn't taken the slightest notice of him, although he had jumped up on to the arm of her chair and mewed a welcome. Oh, she could see how things would turn out: Rosalind and Isabel would be as thick as thieves: they would have private jokes and talk shop incessantly. *She* would be left to pair off with Sophie. . . .

The transfer came through all right; very quickly, about ten days later. Miss Matthews, Rosalind's headmistress, was very gracious and said that she would squeeze Isabel into Lower VA somehow. So there was no need for further delay. The sooner poor Isabel settled down in her new home, the better.

Rosalind was all plans and excitement. Wouldn't Isabel be lonely all by herself in the guest-room? Why shouldn't Isabel share with her?

"Because she's used to a room of her own," said Mrs. Rendell firmly. "Rosalind dear, I know how forthcoming you are, but Isabel . . . You must realize she will feel very strange with us for a time. She's had two big emotional shocks in her life: when Aunt Rachel adopted her—she was only three then—and now this one."

"You mean she may be a sort of problem kid with a chip on her shoulder?"

Jessica raised her head from her painting. She would be only too pleased to resign her rôle of black sheep of the family to someone else for a change. But her mother's reply was disappointing.

"No, Rosalind, I don't mean that. She's very attractive and polite and eager to please. But she was, you know, the very centre of Aunt Rachel's life, and you've only got to see her pretty frocks and her hair to realize she's been brought up like a little princess. I'm afraid that she's bound to go through a difficult time of readjustment. The great thing is to make her feel that this is just as much her home as it is yours."

"Oh, Mum, you leave her to me!" cried Rosalind. "I'll jolly her along and give her no time to mope. Oh, it will be fun having a twin sister!"

But Jessica thought, burying her nose in Claudius's fur: "Isabel will make everything different. Home will be nicer or nastier. Never the same again."

# 4

## *Isabel*

Isabel arrived about a week later, on Sunday morning.

She came shyly into the hall, clasping her tennis-racket and her rain-coat and a small suitcase, while her aunt took the rest of the luggage out of the back of the car. She looked as if she had come out of a band-box instead of a dirty train.

Rosalind cried, "Hullo, Isa!" and seized her racket and her rain-coat. Then Mother came in and made the introductions. "I don't suppose you remember any of your cousins. It's such a long time. . . . This is Rosalind . . . and Jessica . . . and Sophie."

Isabel shook hands nicely with them all. But the only one she really smiled at was Sophie.

"Mum, I'll take her to her room," cried Rosalind. The church bells could be heard ringing, and she said, as she put her arm through Isabel's and guided her up the stairs, "We all went to church early this morning, so that we could get it over and all be back to welcome you."

Jessica hesitated; then followed them.

"Voilà!" cried Rosalind, flinging open a door on a

smell of fresh air and polish. "You've got the new mattress. It's bouncy." She sat on it, and then darted to a tin on the bedside table. "These are biscuits in case you suffer from night starvation."

Jessica hung about in the doorway, the tip of her tongue caught between her teeth. Isabel was gazing about her, helpless. The church bells stopped. The whole world seemed to fall silent.

"If—if you want anything at night," faltered Rosalind, "you have only to tap on the wall by your bed. My bed is just the other side of it. You will feel like the Count of Monte Cristo."

Something brushed Jessica's sleeve. It was Sophie. She had crept up too, another silent observer.

As if three pairs of eyes were more than she could stand, Isabel moved across to the window and looked out.

"What a lot of trees," she said.

Rosalind came up and put a hand on her shoulder.

"We're awfully lucky. Our garden used to be part of a big estate. The old avenue leading to the Manor runs along the bottom of the garden and all those trees you see on the other side of it are a wood. The Manor has been empty now—oh, for about two years—the owner's in Australia—so Jess treats the avenue as more or less her own domain and plays Red Indians there or something."

"I don't!" burst from Jessica.

Isabel turned round. But it was Sophie her eye fell on, still staring at her, silent, from the door. She took in the big grey eyes and black lashes, the smooth creamy cheeks and little rounded chin.

"Isn't your little sister pretty," she said.

Jessica frowned. Mum didn't like people saying that in front of Sophie in case it turned her head. Of course Mum didn't realize that Sophie had been *born* with her head turned; it didn't really matter what was said. She could see Rosalind was about to come out with one of her "*pas devant les enfants*" utterances, when their mother's voice floated up the stairs:

"Rosalind, don't keep Isabel up there talking. Coffee's ready!"

Isabel was shy; but what with Rosalind being such a chatterbox and Mother so kind and Father ready with his funny little stories, the morning passed off all right. At lunch-time she proved helpful. She was always ready to spring to her feet if there were plates to clear or dishes to fetch from the kitchen. Jessica noticed this with gratification. It might mean that she could permanently sit back at meal-times without Rosalind suddenly going on strike and proclaiming, "Mum, it's always me! Jess doesn't do a thing."

In the afternoon it was decided that Rosalind and Jessica should take their cousin for a walk in the park. They stood by the artificial lake watching the mallards breasting through the water, very quiet. Rosalind, of course, had to relate the story of how Jessica had once fallen into the water, been fished out by the park attendant and carried into the ice-cream parlour where she had been given a free cup of tea. Isabel frowned and said, "How beastly for her," and stared at the little island in the middle of the lake. It was covered by a thick tangle of bushes and little trees and had a hushed, very secret look.

"It's like the Lake Isle of Innisfree," said Jessica loudly.

"Do you like poetry?" said Isabel.

"Oh, Jes hates it," cried Rosalind. "She's a thorn in Mum's flesh. 'Innisfree' is the one poem she happens to know. . . ." Then she broke off to whisper, "Ssh! . . ." went poker-faced for a minute, and then exchanged polite greetings with a tall lady who passed them with a dog. "Isabel, did you *see* her? That's our Miss Matthews!"

This encounter with her head-mistress set Rosalind's tongue really wagging. She chattered away about school, and gradually the stiff, sad look on Isabel's face melted a little and she actually began to ask questions. Jessica found herself falling behind.

"It's just as I thought: they'll be as thick as thieves . . ."

Once or twice Isabel looked round at her. The second time she did this, Jessica said, in a loud voice:

"We'll all go and have an ice-cream."

Rosalind stopped in her tracks.

"Who's paying?"

"I am."

"Don't be silly. You can't afford ice-cream for three."

"I say I can."

Resolutely Jessica led the way to the Ice-cream Parlour, and the two girls followed her. The parlour was crowded, but Jessica spied one empty table and rushed towards it, and said quickly to the waitress leaving the next table:

"Three sixpenny tubs, please."

"No sixpenny tubs sold at the tables. Nothing less than a shilling."

"All right. Three shilling ones," said Jessica, desperate.

How was she to get out of this scrape? She had only got two shillings in her pocket.

"I say, Jessica, ——" Isabel's blue-green eyes were staring straight into hers, a bit scared,—"I'd much rather eat a tub walking along. Honest."

"Same here," cried Rosalind. She could read her sister's face, and felt sorry for her. "Quick, let's go. We'll cancel the order on our way out. I haven't a sou on me."

Jessica crimsoned violently. They all rose, and Rosalind nipped ahead to intercept the waitress, while Jessica, shamefaced, led the way to the counter and fumbled amongst her coppers and threepenny bits. Alert for further disaster, her sister tried to see into her purse, but Isabel, very tactfully, looked the other way.

They ate the tubs walking along. Jessica felt bad. Anybody could see that Isabel, from her film-star hair to her beautiful sandals, had never done anything so common in her life before.

After tea there was one rather blank and awkward moment. Conversation suddenly dried up, and Isabel, Jessica noticed, looked as if she were just about to cry. Then, suddenly, she said, in a very small voice:

"Aunt Lydia, what time does your Sunday post go?"

"Five-fifteen. Oh, Isabel, I was forgetting . . . I did ring up Mrs. McMillan to say you'd arrived safely, but, of course, she'll be looking out for a letter. You've just time. . . ."

"I did promise Maimie . . ."

Isabel broke off confused; and Jessica, staring, had a

sudden picture of a train moving off out of a station and a girl called Maimie, crying out, as she ran beside it, "If you find your beastly cousins absolutely ghastly, mind you come back to me!"

It was extraordinarily vivid.

Mother asked tactfully if Isabel would like to write her letter quietly in another room. Isabel replied that she would be all right here, thank you. She had a writing-case with her initials on it in gold. Jessica watched her write the address and the date and then stare out through the window at the houses opposite. She got out her handkerchief and blew her nose very discreetly. A weight fell on Jessica's heart. She knew that Isabel was hating everything: the view from the window, the room about her, the five strange people to whom she had somehow got to grow accustomed. . . .

Sophie tiptoed lightly up to her mother. She whispered something in her ear.

"Yes, *lovely*, darling. I'm sure Isabel would like it. Just as soon as she's finished her letter and come back from the post."

Jessica pulled a face. She knew what all that meant: "The Pied Piper", sure as fate.

For years and years the family had all been expected to down tools and gather round when Sophie offered to recite. This hadn't been too trying when the poems were short ones, such as "I love little pussy"; but "John Gilpin" and "High Tide on the Coast of Lincolnshire" went on and on and on. Jessica could admit that Sophie was good, but adulation wasn't good for Sophie. She had far too much of it. And now here she was, on Isabel's very first evening, standing up in front of them and collecting all their eyes as she gave out the title:

" 'The Pied Piper of Hamelin'."

Then she was well away. . . .

After that she offered to recite "Toll for the Brave". Perhaps Mum thought that this wasn't a very cheery choice; anyhow she tactfully pointed out that Isabel must be very tired and have had enough for one evening.

At eight o'clock Isabel looked so white and tired that Daddy suggested she should go early to bed.

Mum had already seen that Isabel had everything she wanted, but that didn't prevent Rosalind from bustling after her, patting the eiderdown, rearranging the curtains and asking if she could try on Isabel's exotic silk dressing gown.

Once again Jessica hovered in the doorway, scowling under her fringe.

Isabel had unpacked by now. There were little bottles on her dressing-table, very neatly arranged, a Bible on the table by her bed, and on the mantel-shelf were two photographs in silver frames. And—Jessica sniffed—there was a faint, flowery smell in the room already.

Chattering, Rosalind advanced to the mantel-shelf. Luckily she omitted to make any remark about the photograph showing Uncle Graham, Aunt Rachel and Isabel, standing close together, arms linked, and turned all her attention on the photograph of a tomboyish girl in jodhpurs, hands braced behind her, the wind blowing her hair.

"I say, who's that?" demanded Rosalind.

"Maimie."

You could see, hear, that Isabel hated nosiness. She was a secret person, with secret thoughts of her own.

And you could see that she didn't awfully like Rosalind.

*Would* they be able to make her happy again?

# 5

# *The Poster*

The strange thing was that everything seemed much as usual again by Monday morning. Jessica lay in bed hearing water running, feet pattering, doors banging; she felt the concentrated silence in the room as Sophie wrestled with the parting in her hair. There was also a nice smell of coffee and frying bacon.

"Jess!"—Rosalind poked her head in at the door. "Mother says you're to get up at once!"

Isabel sat next to Sophie at breakfast. Jessica, eyeing her across the table, noticed that she didn't eat much; she looked excited and scared and a bit bewildered. She wore one of Rosalind's school gingham frocks pulled in round the waist and looked nicer than Rosalind did in hers. When breakfast was over she jumped up to help clear away.

"Don't you bother about that, dear," said Mother. "Rosalind likes to be the first person to arrive at her school every morning and Jessica likes to be the last person to arrive at hers. And as Jessica's school is quite close, she has a good ten minutes to spare after you and Rosalind have gone. It doesn't hurt her to clear the plates for me."

Jessica glared at her mother. What a way to put it. She stood at the window, slowly drawing the marmalade spoon down her tongue, as she watched Rosalind and Isabel going out through the front gate; Rosalind talking nineteen to the dozen.

"Jess, do hurry up with the tray, dear!"

But Jessica rarely hurried when she was told to. She was like a clock whose regulating device was set the wrong way. Ten minutes later she was in a state.

"Mum, have you taken my history book?"

"Why on earth should I take it, dear?"

"Because you look inside to see if I've done it properly and then put it down in some funny place."

"Nobody has touched your book, Jessica."

Jessica rushed back into the dining-room, and savaged the newspapers and cushions, which she had already disarranged in her initial search. The clock struck a quarter-to-nine.

"I shall be late!"

Mrs. Rendell very calmly found the book in her satchel, jammed inside her atlas. With a smothered cry Jessica rushed out of the house. The road was empty. No straw boaters were walking in one direction, no red berets in the other. It was ominous, like the moment before a crack of thunder. If you were late you were kept in for forty minutes after school on Fridays.

She ran all the way. The vast, prison-like cloakroom was almost empty. She ran with pounding heart along the corridors and reached the closed door of 11A classroom. She walked in.

There was complete silence. Mr. Berryman, seated at his desk, had broken off what he was saying. Everybody, seated quietly in their places, stared too.

Feeling awful, Jessica walked towards her desk, and as she did so, Mr. Berryman spoke.

"Jessica, we were just talking about you."

Mr. Berryman was Jessica's form-master. He was a heavily-built man, with small beady eyes. He did not look particularly nice, but he was nice. Unfailingly kind and always cheerful, he would throw himself down on to one of the ordinary school chairs without ever a thought that it might crack beneath his fourteen stone. He waited now for the nine o'clock bell to stop shrilling along the corridors, and spoke again.

"We all think you ought to do that poster for us."

"What poster?"

Mr. Berryman looked into Jessica's very clear blue eyes and realized that she hadn't the faintest notion what he was talking about.

"Jessica, are you one of those awful children who never read the school notice-board?"

Jessica sat rigid with her toes digging hard into the floor.

"For the last week there's been a big poster on it about the 'Freedom from Hunger' Talk on Friday afternoon. The poster *also* says that each form is asked to make its own poster. Then, on Friday, there is to be an exhibition of them. The form all think that you ought to do the one for us."

"Me! Really?"

"Yes, you. Really."

The form tittered. But there were also cries of: "Go on, Jess, you do it for us!" "Jess is smashing at painting!" "I think Jess is as good as Michael Angelo!"

Jessica glowed all over with gratification, and had to keep her eyes fixed hard on Mr. Berryman, in case her face showed it too much. During Art class, people often crowded round her easel and made remarks which could be interpreted as admiring, and Miss Giles had been known to say, "That's coming on nicely, Jessica." But nobody had ever said anything like this outside the studio before. Her fame had spread.

"You go along to Miss Giles at 'break', and ask her for some cartridge paper," said Mr. Berryman, as if that was that.

Jessica, accordingly, presented herself at the studio. Miss Giles was busy, assembling a grotesque collection of bones, dead branches and rocky stones for her next class, but she readily left it all to produce a large sheet of white paper, some rough sugar-bag sheets for trying out ideas on, and some poster paints. Jessica lingered, giving her every opportunity to say, "I shall expect something very good from you," but all she said was: "Now—anything else?"

Jessica staggered back to her class-room with the booty and arranged it all on top of her desk. She loved little jars of paint.

Mr. Tomkins, the History master, stared, testily.

"What's that enormous roll of paper doing on your desk? *And* all that impedimenta? Put it away, put it away. Put that roll of paper on the floor."

Tomcat was not to be trifled with. Unwillingly, Jessica placed the roll of paper close to her own feet, casting a glance of hatred at Bunny Bulsher in the neighbouring desk. His great feet never seemed properly attached to his legs. They'd kick out and leave a grey imprint of composition sole on her paper, sure as fate.

She walked home in a dream.

The first thing she heard when she got inside the house was Rosalind jabbering away to Isabel. Isabel . . . She had forgotten everything about her.

Rosalind said: "Someone asked if we were twins. We're both so fair, and the same height."

Jessica glanced from one to the other. Rosalind was ruddy and golden, with round cheeks and round blue eyes and very curly lashes. Isabel was slim and blonde, with high cheek-bones; and her eyes hadn't Rosalind's little-girl stare.

After tea, she waited until her mother was out of the way, and then nipped into the kitchen for the pastry-board. When she returned to the dining-room Rosalind and Isabel were standing one on each side of Sophie, admiring her book of sums.

Jessica swiftly staked her claim at the table. The pastry-board was set up against Rosalind's fat dictionary, and the sugar-paper was pinned to it. Then she lovingly set out her pencils, rubber, charcoal, poster-paints, and a white plate for mixing her colours on. Oh, bliss. Jessica's fingers, all delicacy, hovered over her paints.

"Jessica Rendell, what are you doing? And that's my dictionary!"

"A 'Freedom from Hunger' poster," said Jessica, in a

shutting-up voice. She was aware of both girls staring at her, and she seized a pencil.

But Rosalind did not mean to shut up.

"Do you call that homework?"

"I call it school work,"

"Who asked you to do it?"

"Mr. Berryman."

"Only you?"

Jessica was careful not to boast.

"I did not hear him ask anyone else."

"Is it for a school competition or something?"

"I don't know."

Rosalind turned to Isabel. "If you ask Jess anything about school, she always says she doesn't know."

"Well, I *don't* know."

"Now, look here, Jess," said Rosalind, in very reasonable tones, "you can't do it here; there's no room. Can't you take everything into the kitchen?"

"No, I can't."

"She's as obstinate as a mule," said Rosalind to Isabel.

Jessica flushed. She was being made to appear difficult in front of Isabel, who sat there so cool and critical, taking sides against her.

Mrs. Rendell came in.

"Why, Jessica, when did I say you could take my pastry-board?"

Jessica, aware of Rosalind's triumphant glance, said nothing.

"And why aren't you doing your homework?"

"Mr. Berryman asked me to do a poster."

"Oh, Mother," said Rosalind, "it's only a 'Freedom

from Hunger' poster; and if you ask Jessica anything about it, she'll just say, 'I don't know'."

"I'm not asking your opinion, Rosalind. . . . Now, Jessica dear, you get your arithmetic and history done first."

"Then you'll say I've got to go to bed."

"My dear child, it's only half-past five. Now take that great board off the table and allow Isabel a little more room. In fact, I think it would be a good idea if you set it up in Rosalind's bedroom and worked at your poster there."

"But Mother, I'm taking Isabel up there to listen to my pop records," expostulated Rosalind.

"Aunt Lydia," said Isabel shyly, "couldn't Jessica use my room? I've got all that big room to myself, while Jessica and Sophie have to share."

"But you have no idea how untidy Jessica is," said Mrs. Rendell smiling.

"Frightful!" cried Rosalind. "Oh, Mum, it really would be ever so much better if Isa moved into my room and shared with me. Then Jess could have the spare room all to herself and be as messy as she likes. She could stick her easel by the window and get all the light."

Isabel flushed. She looked distressed, and her lips parted.

"No, Rosalind," said Mrs. Rendell, very firmly. "But since Isabel's kindly offered Jessica her room to do her poster in—well, what about it, Jessica? Can you promise to stack everything up neatly before you leave it? All right, then; take all that stuff up now, and then as soon as you've done your prep. you can go and get started."

"I'll help you," said Isabel. She seized the wastepaper basket and quickly arranged the paints and brushes securely while Jessica struggled with the pastry-board and the rolls of paper.

As soon as Isabel had helped to move the dressing-table and cleared it by putting her own things into a drawer, she left Jessica to set out everything in readiness on her own.

* * *

The poster was finished on Wednesday evening. The family gathered round it in Isabel's bedroom. Jessica had a smudge of charcoal on her nose and filthy nails; but the poster was spotless.

"It is very good indeed, darling," said Mrs. Rendell. "I like your school-girl feeding a black baby out of a bowl."

"I suppose it's you," said Rosalind. "She's got your slippery brown hair. *And* your Alice band."

"I wish I could draw like that," said Isabel. "Jessica's awfully clever, isn't she?"

There was a rather surprised silence.

"Jessica has certainly a talent for painting," said Mrs. Rendell.

Jessica gave her mother a peculiar look. Painting didn't count. People in nut-houses painted. Gorillas painted. There had even been an exhibition of chimpanzees' paintings in London.

"Oh, Jess can paint you anything you like," said Rosalind. "And now, perhaps, we can have some pastry again."

"Yes, darling, I should like to have my pastry-board back," said her long-suffering mother.

Jessica took her poster to school the following morning. As she waited to cross over, Nance turned the corner out of her council-house road, and ran along the opposite pavement, waving.

"Take care!" she called.

But Jessica did not mean to run any risks with her poster. At a safe moment she darted across to her friend.

"What you got there?" demanded Nance.

"My poster."

"Oh, that!"

Jessica was taken aback. However truculent Nance might be to others, she was unfailingly nice and kind to her. Why had she snorted?

"I won't show it to you, if you don't want to see it."

"'Course I want to see it, if you done it! Show us."

Jessica stopped dead, unrolled her poster, and held it out for comment.

"Why, Jess, that's real good! But ——" and Nance broke off to shake her head—"that poor little black won't even get one tiny dollop of that gruel you're ladling out to him."

"You do like it, though?"

"I said I did. It's smashing. I just don't like what it's *for*."

Jessica could see that she wasn't going to get any more aesthetic appreciation out of Nance. She rolled up her poster.

"What do you mean—what it's *for?*"

"If you'd read last Sunday's paper, you'd know well enough."

"Well, I didn't."

"There was this great blurb. 'Champagne with Funds for Starving. African Bridegroom's Drunken Orgy while Children Starve.' You should have heard my Dad go off the deep about it! 'That's what happens to all our money screwed out of us by these house-to-house collectors,' he said."

Mum was a collector. Jessica said, bewildered:

"Are you sure?"

"It was in black and white."

"But the Society wouldn't ——"

"The Society sit on their bottoms all day in offices, typing out receipts and sticking on stamps. They don't know what happens to the funds once they reach Africa."

Jessica said nothing.

"Charity begins at home: that's what I say," said Nance. "What about our old-age pensioners?"

"What about them?" asked Jessica timidly. Nance spoke as if it were her fault.

"Most of them are half-starving."

"But—but isn't there something called . . ."

"National Assistance. Do you know what the National Assistance man said to old Ma Rogers?"

"No."

" 'Mrs. Rogers, this five shillings a week extra I'm giving you, is to pay for *your* milk, not the cat's. Get rid of the cat!' "

"Oh, Nance . . ." Oh, Claudius . . . She would rather starve than turn Claudius out into the street. . . .

"Yes, I could tell you some tales!"

"Don't. . . . Nance, are you quite sure—I mean about our collections being used for drunken orgies?"

"Kid, I wouldn't have you on. Easy though it would be. I was right about that policeman, wasn't I? Right about there having been a ——"

"Yes, yes, I know."

"I reckon I've got a bit of second-sight. My Dad's Gran had it."

"You mean, you have a kind of vision of our money being used for drunken orgies?"

Nance hesitated. "What I mean is: why *shouldn't* you believe me?"

Jessica glanced up at her tall friend. Like Mr. Berryman's, her face wasn't all that prepossessing: her nose was too long and thin, her eyes too small. Yet, somehow, she liked and trusted it.

"But what can *we* do?"

"Well, for a start, I don't hold with this jaw on Friday."

"Will you tell Mr. Berryman?"

"I would quick enough if he'd listen to me! But," cried Nance, with sudden passion, "nobody *will* listen to me! You know how they all shut me up! *He'd* just wangle me around and jolly me along and before I knew where I was I'd be stuck in the hall on Friday along with the rest of you. It's no good *saying;* we must *do*."

"We?" said Jessica, nervous.

"Well, two would be better than one. Make more of a demonstration."

"How?"

"Oh, just sit ourselves down somewhere like the 'Ban the Bomb' people."

"I *couldn't* do that! We'd get into awful trouble."

"We've got to sit somewhere, if we're not sitting in the hall."

Jessica looked more and more uneasy.

"Look, kid, this Talk isn't like a lesson. Who's to notice if we're not there? But you please yourself."

"I thought you meant a real demonstration."

"It is a real demonstration. We prove what we feel about it by staying out of the lecture. I'm not suggesting you and I parade about the school with placards on us."

"Oh, I see . . ."

"Anyhow," finished up Nance, for they had arrived at the school gates, "I'm not going to listen to a half-hour's jaw on feeding the hungry goodness-knows-where, when I know of one poor old thing practically next door, with nothing in her larder but a tin of cat's food."

"Truly?"

"Cross my heart."

No more was said on the subject for the time being. Jessica carried her poster into the class-room, and was soon asked to show what she had done. She unrolled it, and an admiring crowd gathered round. Even Pete Sangster, who was very tough and jeered at everything, stared at it almost reverently.

"I like that little black feller in the vest."

Jessica could feel herself swelling with pride. But one quick glance at Nance sitting in her desk, legs stuck out, arms folded and an inscrutable look on her face, deflated her fast enough.

Then Mr. Berryman blundered in, shouting, "Good

morning, good morning!", flung himself down in his chair which shuddered beneath him, and observed the crowd. "Ah, the poster! Bring it along, Jessica. Let's have a look at it."

Jessica willingly complied. Even if Mr. Berryman thought that the poster was awful, he would find something encouraging to say. Unlike Miss Giles, he never made one the reluctant observer of imperfections which one had failed to notice oneself.

"Why, this is first-rate, Jessica. First-rate. And what I call a clever piece of propaganda. Your little school-girl feeding that black baby ought to swell the collection all right."

There was a loud snort from Nance.

Mr. Berryman must have heard. And had he said, "And what does that noise signify?" a great deal of trouble would have been avoided. But the staff had learnt to be wary of Nance by now. Her opinion was the last they wished to hear on *any* subject.

"Leave your poster with Miss Giles some time," said Mr. Berryman, "and she will stick it up in the hall with the others."

Jessica walked back to her desk. Nance was looking at her, she knew; but for the life of her Jessica couldn't meet her stare. She felt in some obscure, muddled way that she had taken advantage of something she didn't believe in to collect plaudits for herself. Her poster was a lie. The little black baby wasn't going to be fed by the boys and girls of Westbridge Secondary Modern. The collection would be used for drunken orgies . . . and *he* would go hungry.

At "break" she took her poster along to the studio. Miss Giles was alone and pinning up a painting on the wall. On any other occasion Jessica would have hovered around for a bit in the hope that Miss Giles might at last come out with something about her genius. Now all she did was to tiptoe up to Miss Giles's desk, place her poster on it and tiptoe off again.

Then she joined Nance at the milk-hatch.

"I'm not going to that Talk tomorrow."

Nance gaped. Her sharp, ginger-coloured eyes suddenly looked very nice and concerned.

"Sure, kid?"

"Quite sure."

# 6

# *Mr. Stephens and Jessica*

It was, of course, a ghastly idea. Jessica did not look forward to the demonstration one little bit. Nance, on the other hand, appeared completely unconcerned. At dinner-time she settled down to her plate of apricot tart and custard as if all she had in mind was the hope of a second helping.

"What do we do when dinner is over?" Jessica whispered. "Where do we go?"

"Mmmmm? Oh, nothing. Just follow me."

The master in charge said "grace". He also said that the school would be allowed twenty minutes in which to digest their dinner, then a bell would ring and they were all to come AT ONCE to the Assembly Hall. The talk would begin at one-forty SHARP.

Jessica felt weak at the knees. But Nance, whistling, joined the crowd of boys and girls surging out into the playground. She stood close to the school wall, gazing up at the sky. Then, suddenly, she grabbed Jessica's wrist.

"This way."

Keeping close to the wall, they skirted a wing of the

building, all huge glass windows showing the empty laboratory inside, turned another corner and reached the bicycle-shed.

"Here we are. We'll lie doggo in here until the bell rings. Cripes, you look scared!"

The bicycle-shed smelt strongly of rubber tyres and added to Jessica's feeling of being where she had no business to be.

"I *am* scared!"

"What you scared about, eh? Nobody's going to take a roll-call before the Talk!"

The bell rang. It sounded a bit far away from the bicycle-shed. But they could hear a surge of feet and babble of voices as the boys and girls converged upon the school door. Then there was silence. Complete silence.

"Come on," said Nance.

"Aren't we going to stay here?"

"Not me! I'm going to lie down in the shade of the trees and have forty winks."

"We'll be seen!"

"Seen? Who by? They're all shut up in the hall by now."

"But what about the Staff? They sit out on the roof balcony during the dinner-hour. We've often seen them."

"Oh, I'm not worrying about them. If they choose to stop away from the talk, why shouldn't we?"

"I'm not crossing the grass with them watching!" cried Jessica vehemently.

"Look, kid, if you're nervous, I'll have a squint up at the balcony. If nobody's sunning themselves we'll scoot across the cricket pitch to those trees. It'll only take us two jiffs."

Calm as you please, Nance walked out backwards from the shed, gazing up. Above her head to the right was the open sun-roof which was part of the staff's sacred domain.

"Not a soul," she hissed. "Come on."

Jessica hung back, but Nance snatched at her wrist, held it in a grip of iron and pulled. Nance's legs were long. Jessica felt she had never run so fast in her life before. The grass was a blur under her feet. Panting, she all but fell on her face when they reached the trees.

"Gee, I made you run too fast. Relax, kid," said Nance. She stretched herself flat, hands locked behind her head. "My, this is what I call a heat-wave. If it gets very much hotter, I shall be like a dog with fleas. Frizzling heat don't suit me."

"Nance, couldn't you bend your knees a bit? They'll be seen, sticking right out like that."

"No, I can't. And who's to see us?" But Nance was good-natured, and obliged. She also took a bar of chocolate out of her pocket and broke it in half.

"Here."

"Oh, Nance, thank you. I'm always eating yours."

"You're welcome." Nance closed her eyes. She said, sleepily, "My word, this is better than being stuck in that hall, listening to bla bla bla."

"Oh, Nance, is that *really* why we're here?"

Nance raised her heavy lids for a second. She said firmly:

"I'm here on *principle*."

A moment or two ago Nance's knees made acute

angles; now they were flat out again in the full glare of the sun, and she was snoring her head off. Jessica gazed shrinkingly about her. Such easy unconcern on the part of her friend had a mixed value. It was reassuring only until you began to wonder how safe it was to be with anyone so completely unable to see that things could go wrong.

But all was calm, green and silent. Two white butterflies jigged crazily round each other. They made no sound, and when they vanished into the glare of the sky, the silence merged into the stillness. . . .

Jessica thought of the stuffy hall.

"It is quite nice out here, isn't it!"

"Mmmmmmm."

"This must be a very old chestnut tree. If you look up through all those layers and layers of leaves, you can feel how old it is."

"Hmmm."

"I wish I knew a nice poem about a tree."

Drowsily, Nance began to sing.

"Under the spreading . . . chest . . . nut tree . . ."

"I mean a real poem, like 'Sea Fever' or 'Innisfree'."

"I thought you didn't like poetry."

"I *can't* like it altogether when Mother *wants* me to like it."

"Aren't you funny!"

Jessica didn't mind being called funny by Nance because of the nice way she said it.

An express train roared through the cutting beyond the football field. Nance yawned and drew up her legs beneath her.

"That's the two-fifteen. I think we ought to be scouting round so that we can nip in with the crowd when they leave the hall."

"Oh, Nance ——" Jessica jumped to her feet—"we must hurry."

"Now just keep calm."

So saying, Nance seized Jessica's hand and ran with her across the exposed cricket pitch, back to the greater protection of the school building. They followed it round, keeping close to the walls, until they came to a door which led in from the tennis courts.

"In here," said Nance.

They crept inside. The corridor was empty; and because they couldn't hear a sound from anywhere, the whole building might have been empty. Still holding Jessica's hand, Nance led the way. The first corridor led to another, and that, in turn, to the main corridor. At the end of this, wide shallow steps led to a big, square vestibule, with two other staircases on each side leading down to it, and the two double doors of the assembly hall on the far side.

Now they could hear, like a shadow cast over the deep, clear pool of silence, a voice behind the closed doors: a raised lecturing voice going on and on.

"Nance, what do we do now?"

"Wait."

Hardly had the sibilant whisper died away when there came quite a terrifying roar of applause.

Nance pinched Jessica's little finger.

"They'll be out in a sec. Keep back against the wall here, and as soon as we spot our form, we must just dive in amongst them, see?"

Jessica nodded. But the doors did not at once burst open as they expected. They heard instead the Head's voice; then some clapping, that turned weakly into a thin trickle and was lost in a sudden excited buzz of chatter. A voice called for order and a moment later came the rattle and scrape of hundreds of chairs as the audience rose to their feet. Then all in an instant both the swing doors shot forward and a mob of boys and girls hurtled out.

Discipline appeared to have broken down somewhere. The vestibule was packed with a flood of humanity, of whom it seemed that each separate individual had determined on going a way different from the rest. Nance stood on tiptoe, straining for a glimpse of their form-mates. She spotted several of them on the other side of the vestibule, battling their way to the far staircase and dwarfed by a gang of fourth-form boys. There was no point in trying to join them.

"Come on. Up this way!" cried Nance.

Jessica wanted to hold back. The near staircase filled her with even greater alarm, for here an entire class, having swarmed up the stairs ahead of everyone else, had realized that it had left its books behind and was now shouldering its way down through the apparently solid mass that was struggling up. People had been known to be squashed to death in crowds, trampled underfoot. But Nance had already fought her way in, and so she ducked her head and blindly followed her.

At the head of the staircase the outraged voice of Mr. Tomkins demanded order. The roar ceased abruptly. Jessica walked along the upper corridor in decent calm, and arrived at her class-room.

She realized as soon as she entered that she was causing something of a sensation, but Mr. Tomkins was hard on her heels, and as soon as he appeared there were cries of: "Here she is, Mr. Tomkins!" "Mr. Tomkins, look! Jessica's come!"

"Yes, yes," said Mr. Tomkins testily. He gave Jessica a half-glance, as she, scared out of her wits, slipped into her seat. "Now, we've no time to waste. We've lost ten minutes of this lesson already. Get out your big folders. And, Jessica, just run along to Mr. Stephens and tell him you're found. Cut along."

"Found . . .?"

"Quickly!"

"Just me?"

Mr. Tomkins ignored the question. He was unfurling a huge chart he had prepared showing the movements of population in the nineteenth century, and Jessica no longer existed for him. Stupefied, Jessica walked towards the door and opened it.

As she turned to shut it behind her she had a vision of Nance, bolt-upright in her desk, mouth open, staring after her.

Jessica walked slowly along the corridor. During her five-and-a-half terms at Westbridge Secondary Modern she had never had a private interview with her headmaster. She knew where his room was, and that he had an arrangement of coloured lights on his door. Mr. Stephens's red light meant "engaged", his yellow light meant "out", his green light meant "in". She arrived, quaking, at his door, and there was the green light, fixing her with its eye. Very timidly she knocked, inclined her ear to the panelling; and heard nothing. There was nothing for it: she knocked more loudly.

This time a bell rang from inside. She opened the door.

Mr. Stephens was a thin man with black hair and blue eyes. Dynamic when addressing the whole school, he was just the opposite when alone with one child. He thought before he spoke, stared a lot, and seemed dissatisfied with what he saw.

His first words were not even addressed to Jessica, but to his secretary who was hesitating by an open door on one side of the room.

"Miss Smith, just get that number again, will you? Tell Mrs. Rendell she has turned up and that there's nothing to worry about. I'll speak to her myself after I've had a word with Jessica. Now, Jessica . . ." Mr. Stephens paused, thought hard as he moved an object on his desk, and then settled himself for a long stare at his pupil—"I want you to tell me first of all where you have been for the last hour?"

"Out . . . in the grounds . . . under the chestnut trees."

"I see. Now can you tell me why you weren't in the hall listening to the lecture with the rest of the school?"

Jessica stared back hypnotized into the bright blue eyes. No, she couldn't tell him; not without Nance at her side to do all the explaining. Nance . . .

"Did you think the lecture was going to be very dull? I know we have, unfortunately, had two very dull lecturers this term. Was that your reason for not turning up?"

"No. No. That wasn't my reason."

"I see. Suppose you tell me what your reason was then?"

He was trying very hard not to frighten her. She would *have* to say something.

"Because . . . because it didn't seem right to send money to Africa for wedding orgies while there are lots of old people . . . in England . . ."

". . . lots of old people in England? . . . yes?" prompted Mr. Stephens, making Jessica feel like one of those tape measures that spring back into a coil again once you let go.

". . . . starving."

Mr. Stephens did not say "I see" this time. He appeared too surprised.

"Could you tell me where you got this idea from?" he asked.

Jessica hung her head and explored her top lip with the tip of her tongue. She could not, *could* not say, "Nance Parker": that would be telling tales. True, Nance had appeared quite airily indifferent about getting into a scrape; one might even credit her with the wish to advertise her principles. But if that was the case why wasn't she here?

"I don't know."

Mr. Stephens suddenly looked as her father did after a heavy day's work.

"It just came to you, did it? Well, don't you think it would have been much more sensible and polite and all the rest of it, to have come here and given your views to me? This is your school just as much as it is mine. I want to know what you girls and boys think about things. That is what I am here for."

At this point Mr. Stephens leaned back in his chair as if

to give a picture of himself waiting, day in, day out, for just this one eventuality.

Jessica swallowed.

"Suppose we discuss your view-point now," he said, leaning forward again. "I think what you mean is this: that there are hungry people in England and that their needs should be met first?"

". . . before the drunken orgies."

"Jessica, you have evidently got hold of some sensational story from somewhere. But all right: you don't want your money misused, so you didn't turn up at the lecture. And the money for the collection is still in your pocket? Yes?"

"Yes."

"It doesn't strike you that your argument would carry a great deal more weight, if the money *wasn't* still in your pocket? . . . if you'd put it, for instance, in the box for 'Old People's Welfare' in the entrance hall?"

Jessica stared, her mind in a fog. She had followed his argument, but with rather the same sense of bewilderment as when the mathematics master led her step by step to some totally unforeseen conclusion.

"Yes, you see, you must be very careful over a point such as this. People can sound very self-righteous in their reasons for refusing to give to certain charities. 'Charity begins at home' they say, or something like that. But does their charity begin at home? Or do they just keep their money in their own pockets?"

Jessica crimsoned to the roots of her hair. She hoped that Mr. Stephens would fail to notice this and would go on playing with a pencil which he had picked up.

"There is just one other point," he continued. "You didn't think it was—well, just a bit shabby to enter for the prize competition when you held such a poor opinion of the fund which was sponsoring it?"

". . . prize competition?"

"Jessica, do you go about with your eyes shut?"

Yes, she did sometimes go about with her eyes shut. Once she had walked right from the lake in the park to the bowling green without opening her eyes. But what was the use of saying so?

"The notice about the Freedom from Hunger Talk was on the notice board in the entrance hall for over a week. If you had read it properly you would have seen that a prize was offered for the best poster advertising the talk."

Mr. Stephens had had his say. Quietly, gently, scathingly, he had reduced Jessica to something very small indeed. Now he put down the pencil which he had been playing with and picked up a book instead.

"You happened to win the prize, Jessica."

"Oh, no . . ."

"You had better take it now, as you weren't in the hall when your name was called out. That was the only reason why we discovered you were missing: you didn't come up to the platform. It's yours: take it."

Holding her prize as if it were a delayed-action bomb and might explode any minute, Jessica returned to Mr. Tomkins's lesson. It was now nearly over. She only had to sit for ten minutes, deaf and miserable, before Mr. Tomkins took himself off and Nance pounced down on her.

"Jess! You did explain it was all my idea, didn't you?"

"'Course I didn't!"

"Oh, Jess! I begged Mr. Tomkins to let me go after you, but he wouldn't listen. He said that you were the one who had been reported missing and you were the one Mr. Stephens had asked to see. You know what he's like. He hadn't been to the talk himself. All he cares about is having enough time to get us going on those old charts of his. I'm sorry, Jess."

"It doesn't matter."

"It does matter. I'll go straight to Mr. Stephens at four o'clock and explain."

"Oh, Nance, I shouldn't. He's so—squashing."

"Oh, he won't squash me. I *want* to tell him my point of view. You wait in the cloakroom for me while I shoot off. I'll only be ten minutes."

The afternoon came to an end. Nance shot off. Jessica found herself surrounded by a crowd of boys and girls.

"It wasn't half a joke, Jess. Mr. Stephens calling out, 'Would Jessica Rendell come up for her prize, please,' and you never bobbing up as expected. 'Where is she?' he said."

"Eh, he didn't half look daft waiting for you to bob up."

"I bet he was mad with you, Jess!"

"Oh, he gave you the prize, did he?"

"What is it? Let's have a look."

"Nobody's going to look at it!" cried Jessica. She snatched it up, threw it into her desk, extricated herself from the bunch of children, and ran off to the cloakroom.

She fully expected to have to wait some moments for Nance but, to her utter surprise, Nance was already in the cloakroom. She turned a hang-dog look on Jessica.

"That secretary wouldn't let me see him—the old cat."

"Oh . . ."

"I argued and argued. And she just said, 'Run away, he's busy; he's no time for you now . . .' "

"Oh dear . . ." Jessica felt really sorry for Nance. She was dying to be a trouble-maker, but no one would let her. . . .

They walked home together.

"I'll have another go at him tomorrow, Jess, honest I will. Last thing I meant was to get you into trouble."

"It's all right—really it is."

"If he won't see me, he could be *made* to see me, you know." Nance made her eyes very round and severe. "I've a *right* to be heard. What you call 'free speech'."

"I know, Nance, but they never seem to like you doing it."

"Ah, some folks never like to hear a bit of the truth."

They parted at the corner of the road. Nance was off with a skip and a run. But Jessica walked slowly and reluctantly towards her home.

# 7

# *A Tin of Cat's Meat and a Packet of Tea*

The front door stood open to tempt a current of air into the house. Jessica slipped inside and bolted up to her room. She tidied herself with lingering care and then tiptoed down again. The dining-room door was also open and she could hear voices and catch a glimpse of Isabel at the tea-table. She was just about to go in with as brazen a look as she could muster, when her mother called from the kitchen.

"Is that you, Jessica?"

"Yes."

Jessica was prepared to admit that much, if nothing more.

"Come in here a minute. I want to speak to you."

Her mother was drying a lettuce on a cloth. She looked at Jessica, and said:

"Now I want to hear exactly what you've been up to this afternoon. No, don't close the door; it's too hot in here. Mr. Stephens has just been on the phone again, so I know all about it."

"If he's told you, Mum,—honest, there's nothing more to tell you."

"Oh yes there is. I want to know exactly why you took up this extraordinary attitude to the Freedom from Hunger Campaign?"

Jessica wished that her mother hadn't got such a clear, carrying voice. They'd hear every word in the dining-room. She hunched her shoulders and her lower lip slid forward.

"I'm waiting, Jessica."

"I *told* Mr. Stephens why. Our money never gets to the hungry children. It's all grabbed up by the black chiefs for their wedding orgies."

"If that's what you *really* think, why have you been giving me sixpence of your pocket-money each month for the house-to-house collection?"

"I don't know. Mum, aren't they waiting for that lettuce?"

"You must know, Jessica. And you can also tell me why you tried to wheedle a shilling out of me at breakfast this morning for the silver collection when, apparently, you'd not the slightest intention of ever parting with it."

Jessica flushed. There is nothing like being accused of double dealing to make one *look* guilty.

"I wasn't sure at breakfast that I wouldn't be going to the lecture."

"You seem to have changed your mind about it very quickly. What *made* you change your mind?"

Jessica fixed her eyes on the lettuce. Here was another poser. For although Nance had appeared perfectly willing to take the blame for everything—in fact, she wanted to take it, and was angry because no one would listen to her—it was hardly safe to bring Nance into it. Mother didn't like Nance. . . .

"Now, come along, Jessica, I mean to get to the bottom of this. Someone must have put the idea into your head. Was it that Nance Parker?"

"Oh—if I say 'yes', you'll hate her more than ever!"

"My dear child, I don't hate her."

"You do, or you wouldn't call her 'that'!"

Mrs. Rendell arranged the lettuce on a plate.

"Listen, Jess: I've nothing against Nance, except that she's her father's daughter. No, *not* because he's a dustman, but because he's always got a grievance about something. He's a trouble-maker, and Nance gets her ideas from him."

"Can I go now?"

"No, I want you to understand what I think of all this. I'm thoroughly ashamed of you, Jessica. I never thought you could be talked into anything so small-minded and sententious."

Mrs. Rendell picked up the plate and moved towards the door; so apparently that was that. Jessica followed her, hang-dog, into the dining-room.

All three stared hard as she entered. Jessica didn't mind her own sisters. They both looked a bit hot: Rosalind's blob of a nose had caught the sun and Sophie's dark hair was swept back, damp and streaky, across her brow. But Isabel looked like the Snow Queen; and how she stared.

"I say," said Rosalind. "What's the row? Jess been expelled or something?"

Mrs. Rendell was aware of Jessica's scowling discomfiture. She said quickly and kindly: "Hush; it's all over now."

"Well, perk up, Jess," said good-natured Rosalind. "Have some lettuce before it's all gone."

"I'm not hungry."

"Not *hungry*? After a whole lecture on hunger?"

Mrs. Rendell intervened again.

"Jessica won the prize for her poster."

"Did she now? The clever poppet! Where is it?"

"Yes, Jessica," said her mother. "Show us your prize, dear."

Jessica looked up just sufficiently to see that Isabel was still staring at her: Isabel, who should have taken over the rôle of the black sheep, the "difficult" one; who should herself have been needing the velvet touch and the tactful word. There she sat, so cool, so appraising, so surprised that anyone could behave so badly.

"I can't. I haven't got it."

"Haven't got it? Where is it, then?"

"It's in my desk at school."

"*In your desk at school*!" repeated Rosalind. She gazed dumbfounded at Jessica, and then turned to Isabel.

"Would you believe it! This is the very first time in her life that she's ever got a prize! The very first time! Yet she doesn't even know what it is!"

"Shut up!" muttered Jessica, her shoulders to her ears. "Shut up, shut up!" Then, with all four pairs of eyes fixed on her, she burst into tears.

She was led up to her room with a glass of lemonade and Claudius for consolation.

"It's the heat as much as anything," said her mother, drawing the curtains against the glare.

Jessica wept into Claudius's black silky fur which smelt of clean dust. But he had soon had enough of it. He stiffened, put his ears back, and then made a frantic heave to get out of her clutch.

"Claudius, don't go!"

Once, when Jessica had cried, Claudius had jumped up on her knee and mewed in sympathy. After that, it was natural to look on Claudius as an ally. Now she was not so sure. He trampled across her face, planting a cold-padded and utterly self-concerned paw in her eye, and then sprang down from the bed to yowl in front of the door.

*Nobody* was on her side.

She cast herself back on her bed and reviewed the whole ghastly day. What Rosalind had said was true; never before had she been given a prize. But the bitterness lay in how it had been given. No gracious, smiling celebrity handing it to her over potted palms, no walking back to her seat amidst thunderous applause. No, the prize had been handed to her like a coal of fire, at the end of a row. She had hardly been able to take it into her hand. It was one of those moments when Jessica seemed to have a kind of bird's eye view of herself, very clear and very awful.

She was an awful person. Such was Mr. Stephens's verdict, and such was her mother's. No matter how much one might blame Nance for the whole situation, the fact remained that she hadn't ear-marked her silver collection for any other charity; she hadn't given Nance's old-age pensioner another thought. In some extraordinarily telling way she had been revealed as mean, small-minded, sententious. What beastly things to be! She didn't mind in the least being called lazy and obstinate: the epithets ran off her like quick-silver. But the word "mean". It was like a tight jersey on a hot day that you couldn't struggle out of quick enough.

Jessica tossed about on her bed, getting hotter instead of cooler. Finally she rolled off it altogether.

An idea had come to her. Why hadn't it come to her hours ago, before Mr. Stephens had made his scathing remarks about self-righteousness? Of course she must feed Nance's old-age pensioner and her cat.

Jessica kept all her worldly wealth in a little leather purse under her handkerchiefs in her top left-hand drawer. The purse revealed nothing but a postal order for ten shillings. The postal order was a birthday present from Uncle Richard, who was also her god-father. It was dated March 16th, and as it was only valid for three months from that date, it would have to be changed on Monday. Apart from that, the purse was empty.

She remembered now: she had lent Bunny Bulcher a shilling towards the model aeroplane he was dying to purchase.

She could, of course, cash the postal order tomorrow. But once it was cashed, and worse still, once it was broken into, it would vanish in no time, fair game for anybody who was to say, "Lend us a tanner, Jess." The postal order was for oil-paints and nothing else in the world, and she had been saving up for them far longer than Bunny had been saving up for his aeroplane. Tomorrow, of course, was pay-day. She would receive the five shillings which must cover the church collection, school charities, sweets, comic, and a bit towards Sophie's birthday next month. There would be precious little to spare for the old-age pensioner. The comic and the sweets would have to be sacrificed.

It was a pity she wasn't a careful saver like Sophie, who put a threepenny bit or a sixpence into her china pig every week.

There it stood, enormously stout, on the mantelpiece. My, it weighed a ton. What a pity that Sophie was such an unwilling lender.

Jessica replaced the pig regretfully. She supposed she had better go downstairs again.

Rosalind was helping Isabel with her maths homework. She said, "Hullo, Jess," in subdued and wary tones, so Mother must have told her to be careful what she said. Isabel just looked. It was as if she were wondering at the gulf between herself and the "difficult" member of the Rendell household. Jessica picked up a comic, flung herself into her father's armchair and held the paper in front of her face. Was it only a little over a week ago that Mother had warned them about being nice and tactful to Isabel, that Isabel *might* be a bit of a problem? Alas, it was only too clear that the comic hid the only problem child under the Rendell roof.

But by Saturday morning Jessica had other things to think about. This was the day. The weekly pocket-money was always given out at breakfast, and the two half-crowns which her mother had put by her plate were a concrete reminder of what she had planned to do. She must buy food for Nance's old-age pensioner and take it round to her. And the sooner the better.

Mother had other ideas.

"Where are you off to, Jessica; before you've put clean sheets on your bed *or* done any of your homework?"

"Just out. While it's still nice and cool."

"Well, I'd rather you did your homework while it's still nice and cool. I don't want you telling me in two hours' time that your brains are too hot to think with."

Rosalind and Sophie and Isabel had already made their beds and were sitting round the dining-room table with their books. Sophie, looking like a good little kitten who had never lost a mitten, was underlining nouns in red crayon and adjectives in yellow. This reminded Jessica of something nice which she had to do. Out came a sheet of drawing-paper, her pencil, rubber and ruler. Then bliss descended. . . .

"Jess dear, what are you doing?"

Mother had come in and was looking over her shoulder.

"A plan of a model village."

"Is that your Social Studies homework?"

"In a way. Miss Dickson said we could illustrate our replies."

"Well, suppose you do the reply first. *And* get on with your maths. I don't see your maths book anywhere about."

Jessica narrowed her eyes at her mother's retreating figure and took her maths books out of her satchel. She gazed glumly at the page before her. When it had all been explained yesterday and most of the class had cottoned on to the idea with quite a show of interest, it had passed over Jessica's head. She had made a pattern in eight parts and coloured five green and three red, but what that was supposed to prove she had no idea. "Eight eighths make one complete unit," she read, and her head swam. "Eighths!" you couldn't even say it properly, let alone think about it. She groaned and sighed and muddled along until she heard the front door bang and saw through the window her mother setting out with her shopping-basket. Here was a chance to nip out and do her own shopping. Rosalind was absorbed in explaining to a worried-looking Isabel something about their Latin homework. Quietly, she slipped from the room.

The High Street was a good fifteen minutes' walk away. But if one crossed over and turned down Dudley Road one came to a little corner shop, dusty and old-fashioned, that sold sweets, cigarettes and groceries. Jessica knew the shop well, and the big bottles of boiled sweets at one end of the counter reminded her of being five years old.

"A tin of cat food, please, Mrs. Sears."

Mrs. Sears was one of those elderly people who believe that everything has changed for the worse. This made her a bit sharp.

"I thought your cat turned up its nose at cat food."

"I don't want it for our cat."

"Oh, you don't, young madam?" Mrs. Sears dumped a tin on the counter, and met Jessica's stare.

"And a packet of tea, please."

"What kind?—if it isn't for you, either?"

"The kind we have."

Mrs. Sears's private opinion was that the physiotherapist's brat hadn't improved since she was a little kid just able to stand with her chin on a level with the counter.

"Two-and-seven," she said shortly.

Jessica picked up the tea and looked at the price on it. "Is there anything cheaper?"

"There is: but it won't be what you asked for."

"I think I'd better have the cheapest you've got."

The packet was silently exchanged for a different-coloured one. Jessica placed a half-crown on the counter; the till drawer shot out with a clang, and Mrs. Sears, in her turn, reluctantly parted with a threepenny bit.

Still silent, Mrs. Sears stared hard at Jessica's back-view in its blue jeans, silhouetted for a second in the open doorway of the shop. A little hooligan, and no mistake.

Jessica hid her purchases in her chest-of-drawers and came bounding downstairs again. Rosalind and Isabel both looked up as she sat down at the table.

"Where have you been?"

"Over to Mrs. Sears."

"What have you been buying?"

Jessica picked up her plan of the model village and regarded it with a mixture of criticism and sheer admiration. Rosalind switched her line of attack.

"I suppose you know that you haven't got a single one of your calculations right?"

"You shouldn't go nosing in my book when my back is turned. And they don't have to be 'right': that's an old-fashioned word!"

"Granted. But the whole point is that they should be reasonable, and yours are just nonsense. Jess, I do think you ought to go over them again."

"I will—some time."

"I'll help you," said Isabel eagerly.

"No, Isabel, you mustn't do that," said Rosalind. "She must do them herself."

"But you help me with my maths!"

Jessica grasped her pencil tight and stared from one face to the other. She was silent with pleasure and surprise.

"That's quite different, Isa. You work terribly hard and worry over your work. Jessica couldn't care less: she won't take in anything you explain."

This observation was so palpably true that Jessica felt unable to refute it. But she fixed her eyes on Isabel, and Isabel's eyes blinked back at her in some kind of answer. It was a silent, secret exchange; but quite what it implied neither of them knew.

The morning grew hotter and hotter. Mrs. Rendell drew the curtains to try to keep the house cool.

Rosalind said at lunch, "Isabel and I thought we'd take a boat on the lake this afternoon."

"I shall have to take Sophie into town to buy sandals," said Mrs. Rendell. "What about you, Jessica?"

"Oh, she can come with us if she likes," said Rosalind, "as long as she doesn't fall in."

But at half-past two Jessica professed a disinclination for the lake. Five minutes later, clutching the cat food and tea, she stepped out into the blazing sunshine.

# 8

# *The House Next Door*

Except for one or two passing cars, the road was deserted. The sun beat down on Jessica's head. She felt the top of it gingerly. My, you could fry an egg on it!

She turned into Grove Road, crossed over and turned down Faircroft Road. Nance's house, number 10, was easy to recognize. It had a sky-blue door with a panel of glass in it through which one could see a net curtain in the shape of an x. Over the porch was a hanging basket bright with geraniums. "One of the things Dad picked out of a dust-bin," Nance had remarked, as if the whole house might be full of such treasure-trove. The little gate was sky-blue also, and the brass 10 on it shone with metal polish.

The houses on each side were shabby in contrast. But which had Nance meant by "the house next door"?

Number 12 had faded cretonne curtains at the window, and the paint on the window-frames was cracked and blistered. Number 8 was not just shabby, it looked dirty and neglected as well. There was no gate to it, and empty cigarette packets and sweet papers had blown into the tiny strip of garden. Golden rod and willow herb grew as high as the little bay window, which was shrouded in a lace curtain which perhaps had once been white but was now a kind of browny-grey. Jessica might have wondered if the house was empty. But two unwashed milk-bottles, one very milky-looking, stood in the porch.

Was this witch's hovel the house of the old-age pensioner?

A very strong reluctance to knock at the door made Jessica hesitate. After all, she had no certain proof that this was the house. It could be number 12, which looked, comparatively, so much more inviting. Surely the best thing to do was to knock on Nance's door and find out.

The bell in the porch proved to be a musical one. Jessica could hear it playing a little bell-like tune in the depth of the house. But nobody answered it; nobody. The house was empty.

Well, there was nothing for it: she must pluck up her courage and knock at the door of number 8.

Determination and fright combined made Jessica feel quite dizzy. She took two steps up the path to the door; and then nearly jumped out of her skin. There was a sudden scuffle almost under her feet and a huge tabby cat leapt clawing up the fence, balanced a second on the top, then scooted off.

Thoroughly unnerved by now, Jessica took a hasty step into the porch. She had an awful feeling that someone had been watching her behind the filthy lace curtains. Well, the sooner she knocked and got her errand of mercy safely over, the better.

She heard nothing at first; then shuffling and thumping, and a blurred shape appeared behind the glass panel in the door. The door opened a crack. A wrinkled, suspicious face peered out.

"Watcher want?"

"Good afternoon. I don't want anything ——" Jessica was acutely aware as she spoke of being looked up and down, taken in: her scarlet face, her grimed shirt, her jeans, everything. "I—I just wondered if ——"

"I want no gipsies here. I been watching yer. Go on; get off, get off!"

"I only came ——"

"Get off with yer! Go on, get off, get off."

The voice was cracked and shrill. Frightened, Jessica backed away. She had a confused idea that the curtains of number 6 twitched and a face peered out. How awful to be *seen* being shouted at. She had a wild desire to drop her two packages and take to her heels. But if she did, a cry would be raised: "You've dropped your things!" No, she must try and walk unconcernedly, holding her packages, as if nothing had happened, no one was shouting at her. . . .

Her father was in the front garden, setting out the sprinkler. He had just turned it on, and a little misty jet was already cooling the air where it fell. He looked up when Jessica came in at the gate. Jessica made another effort to adjust her expression quickly, to assume an air of sang-froid.

"Hullo, Pickles! How are you?"

"Fine, Dad."

Mr. Rendell's kind, clever, monkey-brown eyes rested on his daughter.

"You look a real old ragamuffin in those jeans. Better not let your mother see you."

"I'll change."

Jessica dived into the cool of the house. Up in her room she stuffed the tea and the cat food to the very back of her drawer, and then tore off her shirt and her jeans.

At tea-time she appeared in a brown check gingham and her hair lifted back from her ears by an Alice band. When her mother asked how she had spent the afternoon, she said she hadn't been doing anything.

That night there wasn't a breath of air. Jessica lay spread-eagled on the top of her bed. But that didn't help much; the bed felt hot underneath. At the other side of the room she could hear Sophie's regular breathing. Once she stirred and gave a little cough, but five minutes later she was asleep again.

"I am the only one awake in the whole world," Jessica said to herself.

Thunder grumbled a long way off, like a beast refusing to come out of his den. Sheet lightning turned the night for one soundless second into day.

The afternoon's débâcle came back to Jessica. That awful old woman was a witch. Well, not exactly a witch, but any niceness she had ever possessed had shrivelled and died inside her. Mr. Tomkins had once said that nobody was entirely bad. This was difficult to believe when you thought of cruel boys like Syd Bulsher; and it was equally difficult to believe about an old woman who looked at you with such hate. Otherwise, why should you feel the worse for having met them, as if their evil overpowered you?

She was a failure.

Jessica flung herself about. The air seemed to get closer and closer. Oh, what a mercy she had decided against buying liver for the cat; it would be smelling awful by now. That was *one* good thing. If only she could think of something else that was even remotely cheerful. But the future held nothing but a visit to Grandma next day, who didn't approve of her, and school the following day, and she with her sums all wrong. The sums. . . . She had said she would go over them again, but, of course, she hadn't . . . as Rosalind knew.

But suppose she were to do them *now*—prove Rosalind wrong for once. What was the use of lying here, unable to go to sleep? She might just as well be working at her sums by torch-light. Suppose she got them all right for a change. What a surprise for everyone. She would appear like a new person before their eyes. The idea gave her quite an appetite; she would need extra strength to see it through. What about a ginger nut? What about a glass of lemonade out of the fridge?

Jessica flung her legs over the side of the bed. At the same instant the room flashed white, and then there was a most horrific clap of thunder. Jessica's heart thumped and thumped. She waited for a few moments for her courage to return, and then ventured across the room to the door. Very softly she turned the handle and peered out.

The passage was absolutely silent. A low bulb burned there all night, and it showed the four white painted doors fast shut. But that clap of thunder must have wakened someone. If she made the slightest sound, a voice would call angrily: "What are you doing? Go back to bed at once, Jessica!" and then this wonderful new self would be strangled at birth.

There were the stairs just ahead . . . hushed, spookily silent. The smallest creak of a board would sound like gun-shot in the silence. And then, as Jessica hesitated there, her foot hovering over the top step, she did hear a sound, not made by her at all. Someone was crying.

She stopped dead now, and listened. Yes, the sound came from the room next to Rosalind's; Isabel's room. Her heart started to thump very fast again. How lonely and desolate the crying sounded in the absolute silence of the house! What was she to do?

Only one thing seemed possible. Very gently she turned the handle, pushed the door open a crack into darkness.

"Isa! Isa, are you all right?"

The crying stopped, as if frozen. There was no sound now in the darkness of the room, but the echo of her own *strange* voice.

Yet Isabel was there, holding her breath, willing her to go away.

With an awful feeling of having blundered into privacy, Jessica closed the door very, very gently behind her. After all, if Isabel heard no more, she just might imagine she had dreamt it. . . .

Routed, Jessica crept back to bed.

# 9

# *The Quarrel*

On Sunday morning the family went to church at eight o'clock so that they could start off immediately after breakfast for Grandma's.

Jessica did not know what to think about Isabel as long as they were in church. Either she was feeling very holy, or she wanted to avoid being looked at. She was like a nun wrapped in prayer. But at breakfast, when she and Isabel were sitting dead opposite to each other, of course it was obvious. Isabel looked everywhere but at her.

Except just once.

It was at the beginning of breakfast, when her mother said: "I suppose that loud clap woke you all up last night?" that Isabel suddenly shot her a glance. Whatever those blue eyes blinking at her conveyed—was it a plea or a threat?—Jessica simply did not know how to meet it, except with a stare equally enigmatic.

The day was an unsatisfactory one altogether. Gran was one of those autocratic old ladies who believe they have a right to favourites. Rosalind was her favourite. She always greeted her with: "And how's my briar rose" and kissed her warmly on the cheeks. But Sophie and Jessica she only pecked at. Jessica took it quite as a matter of course that Grandma shouldn't like her and quite understood why she didn't approve of Sophie. But Mother could never understand that part. She used to say, "Sophie, aren't you going to recite one of your poems to Grandma?" And Sophie never would.

This time, there was Isabel as well. Grandma, who was Mr. Rendell's mother, had not met her before. She just gave her a peck and then took no further notice of her. So, while Rosalind sat at Grandma's feet on the lawn, chattering to her in her fluent, eager way, the other three were left to wander about the garden together. The garden was large and rambling, with hidden paths behind clipped hedges and a door in a sun-baked wall, leading into the kitchen-garden. Isabel kept disappearing on her own. At first, Jessica would say, "Oh, there you are!" and run up to her. Eventually it dawned on her that Isabel was wanting to avoid her.

And then the next day was Monday. Jessica looked forward to it even less than usual. She would open the lid of her desk, and the prize would confront her. Bitter reminder of everything that had gone wrong.

But at least she would see Nance and be able to question her about the old witch at number 8.

She rushed off earlier than usual, meaning to hang about at the turning until Nance appeared. But Nance was early too. There she was, strolling along on the far side of the crossing while Jessica had to wait to cross over.

The line of traffic seemed worse than usual. Jessica teetered impatiently on the kerb. Then a motorist halted and signalled her across. Jessica waved her thanks and ran.

"Nance! Nance!"

Nance heard her shouts and turned round to wait.

"Oh, Nance," cried Jessica, breathlessly reaching her side. "I went round to your house on Saturday afternoon and rang and rang, but nobody answered."

"Did you?" Nance looked surprised and pleased. "What time?"

"About three o'clock."

"We'd gone by then, Jess. We took a picnic to the Lido. What do you think of my tan? Mum says I look as if I'd covered myself in toasted bread-crumbs."

Jessica cast a distracted glance at her friend.

"I took a packet of tea and a tin of cat food to number 8. She wouldn't take it. She shouted at me and banged the door in my face."

Nance stopped dead and stared.

"Jessica Rendell, what are you talking about?"

"Your starving old-age pensioner. I ——"

"That's not her house!"

This time it was Jessica who looked flabbergasted.

"Not! But, Nance, there was a cat and all!"

"One cat! That one's got a dozen!"

"Does *she* keep a cats' home?" Jessica went on staring, aghast. It was like a dreadful glimpse into her own far-distant future. Oh no . . .

"I don't know what she doesn't keep in that awful place. Fleas and bugs galore. Jess, whatever made you? Mum's tried to help her, but she's beyond help. The

Sanitary Inspector will create one of these fine days, and then she'll be dragged off to a home, poor old trout."

"She said she'd set the police on me. She called me a gipsy."

"I never meant you to go and knock on her door . . ."

"Where did you mean me to go, then?"

"Ma Minchin lives at number fourteen. Mind you, Jess, you mightn't have got a better welcome there—if it *was* Ma Minchin you wanted. You can't go barging about, knocking on strange doors; and you've got to go careful with funny old things like her."

"What did you mean me to do, then?"

"Me? I didn't mean you to do anything."

"Then—then what was the point of telling me about her!"

"I was just stating a fact."

Jessica digested this in silence. Then she burst out again.

"But you made her the reason for our not going to the talk. *She* should have had our collection money!"

Nance looked puzzled, abashed, gentle.

"Well, my Mum does quite a bit for her. She gives her things and does her shopping for her, and never lets on when the prices go up."

"But that's not me!"

"Honest, Jess, I never guessed you'd do anything so cracked. You *do* get ideas in your head."

"It's you that gets ideas, and me that gets into trouble for them. Mr. Stephens—*and* Mother—made me feel I'd been as mean as mean!"

"Jess, I'm real sorry. I did try and make Mr. Stephens listen. He just waved me off."

"I don't blame him. I wish *I* hadn't listened to you!"

Nance was hurt. She glanced at Jessica's angry face, and said as mildly as she could:

"Honest, it never entered my head you'd go and do a daft thing like that."

"It's not a daft thing to take food to starving people."

"All right; it's not daft, then."

They had arrived at the school gates. Nance's kind, cool, reasonable air made Jessica smart more than ever. She felt she had been outmanoeuvred, put in the wrong by the very person who had caused all the trouble.

"I never want to listen to any more of your awful ideas again."

"O.K. If that's how you feel . . ."

Their pegs were sufficiently far apart in the cloak-room to justify any lapse into silence between them. But neither of them felt it to be a natural and easy silence; and by the time they were in the classroom with no further word said, both realized the awkwardness between them.

Nance glanced at Jessica's face. Although her eyes were lowered and a strand of hair fell forward hiding her face, she did somehow look very forlorn and miserable.

"Done yer sums all right, Jess?"

"Of course I've done them."

"I said, had you done 'em all right? This your book? Let's have a look, shall we?"

Jessica was in half a mind to tell Nance to mind her own business. Then she decided to sit silently back in her desk, fold her arms and allow Nance to be as busybody-ing as she liked.

Nance's sharp eyes didn't need to dwell on the book long.

"Why, Jess, you ain't done a single one of these right!"

"I know I haven't."

"And you just mean to sit there, your arms folded. . . . Why, we were doing these sums during our last term at Primary. They're as easy as easy."

"Easy to you."

"You haven't bothered: I can see that. Just because none of us are supposed to be all that bright in this here school, you sit back and pretend to be more stupid than you are. Here, shove along a bit on your seat and I'll help you."

But Jessica was furious. There was far too much truth in what Nance had said for her to be anything else.

"I don't want your help, thank you."

Nance was taken aback. She stared at Jessica and saw too late that her rallying, down-to-earth speech was not a medicine that Jessica could swallow at the moment.

"Please yerself."

Off went Nance leaving Jessica with the feeling that she *must* look pleased now; there was nothing else for it. To fill in an awkward moment, she narrowed her eyes, snatched at her satchel and pretended to be searching for something in its crumby and fluffy depth. Suddenly she lifted a scarlet and astonished face as she found her hand closing on a sixpenny chocolate wafer. Her favourite kind. If Nance had put it there the situation was indeed embarrassing. But she couldn't have: as Nance had looked over her shoulder at her maths book, the satchel had been sprawled on the floor at Jessica's other side, well out of reach.

So who had put it there? Dad, Mum, Rosalind . . .? Impossible.

But who else was there . . . .

# 10

## *Arbutus Unedo*

Jessica had never fallen out with Nance before, and she did not know how to deal with the situation. She was shocked at her own behaviour. If only she'd let Nance help her with the maths! But this was an uncomfortable thought which she immediately pushed out of her mind. Nance was to blame for everything. It was Nance who had got her into hot water, made her the target for Mr. Stephens's biting and blistering words; Nance who had put it into her head to go round to that awful old woman. And then, to add insult to injury, Nance had practically called her stupid; had spoken to her more or less as Mum spoke to her.

Jessica grew quite hot at the thought. Adult criticism from adults was just one of those things one had to put up with; but adult criticism from Nance, her friend, was a shock, an outrage.

Oh well, Mum was right: she had never liked Nance, had never wanted them to be friends. Hadn't she said only a few days ago, "It's her influence I dislike." She was a bad influence. Jessica paused. She was a little unsure of her logic here. "Bad" was not a word her mother had ever used against Nance. But Jessica was in her black and contrary mood when it was impossible to be fair to anyone, either to her mother or to Nance, or even to herself. Indeed, she took quite a bitter pleasure in going over to her mother's side about Nance for the silly reason that Nance had come out with a criticism that was so very like her mother's. It served Nance right. It served her right, not because of the episode over the lecture, not because of the old witch woman, but simply because Nance had for one shocking moment aligned herself on the other side.

So Jessica shared her chocolate wafer with Bunny, and ganged up with his bunch at "break", and walked home from school with him.

She did not feel nice. And she certainly didn't like the way in which she caught Nance gazing at her. It was not so much sorrow or anger as a kind of puzzled surmise.

That was on Monday. By Wednesday the situation was still the same. But on that day came the letter from Uncle Richard.

Mum broke the news when they were sitting round the table at tea.

"I heard from Uncle Richard this morning. He's tired of his hotel and having nothing to do, so he may perhaps come and stay here for a while."

"Oh, goody!" cried Jessica. "Tell him he *must* come here, Mum!"

"Where will he sleep?" asked Rosalind. "In the garage?"

"Oh!" cried Jessica. She had just taken a large bit of a

doughy bun and could say no more for the moment.

"We'll find room for him. We needn't worry about that now," said Mrs. Rendell quickly.

"Oh, Mum! couldn't he have *my* room? Sophie could sleep with Rosalind and I could sleep on the floor down here. Oh, do let me. He is *my* property!"

"What on earth do you mean: he is your property?" interrupted Rosalind sharply.

"Well, he is. He is only your uncle, but he is my godfather as well. I want him to have *my* room!"

"Of all the idiotic reasons. . . . So we're all to come down to breakfast and find you still snoring your head off and the room in a fug. You're the last person ——"

"That will do, Rosalind," said Mrs. Rendell.

Isabel was following the conversation, looking from face to face. Jessica watched her as she said nervously:

"Aunt Lydia, I'm the one who . . . Couldn't I sleep somewhere else, please?"

"Thank you, Isabel dear, but I'm sure we'll think of something so that nobody has to sleep downstairs."

"I've got it!" cried Rosalind. "Put the camp bed for me in Isa's room! Then Uncle Richard can have mine."

Isabel turned scarlet.

"We'll see," said Mrs. Rendell.

"Isabel won't mind," said Rosalind. "It will be jolly good fun for us both. Won't it, old Isa?"

"Of course," said Isabel. And as if she couldn't help herself her eyes met Jessica's.

"Mum, you just haven't listened to my suggestion. And mine was the very first."

"Jessica, there's something I've been meaning to ask

you. What about that postal order? Have you changed it?"

Jessica pressed her lips inwards and raised her shoulders to her ears.

"It looks as if you haven't. Really, Jessica. . . . Go upstairs and get it and let me see the date on it."

Jessica froze. But four pairs of eyes fixed on hers made her make a sudden, quiet dive from the room.

The postal order was right at the back of her drawer with the tin of cat food and the packet of tea. Hot, frightened, Jessica looked at the post-office stamp. Unless a miracle had happened since Sunday . . . . But no, there was the date: March the sixteenth. Slowly she returned to the dining-room.

Mrs. Rendell took the note from her reluctant fingers and glanced at it.

"Hmm. Two days too late. Jessica, I'm extremely annoyed with you. Didn't I remind you about it only last week? But the more I ask you to do a thing, the more determined you become not to do it. Have you nothing to say for yourself?"

"I did mean to change it on Sunday."

"It's shut on Sunday, goose," said Rosalind.

"I *thought* about it on Sunday. In the middle of the night. I . . ." Without glancing at her, Jessica was aware that Isabel had caught her breath. "And then I just forgot," she finished lamely.

"Well, Jessica, if you value money as little as that, you might remember that other people aren't in the position to treat it so lightly. Your uncle hasn't money to throw away, even if you have. . . . Well, it's of no use to anybody now. You'd better tear it up."

"Couldn't she try at the post office? If it's only two days . . ." said Rosalind. "They might not notice the date," she added experimentally.

"Don't put ideas like that into her head. I believe Jessica to be honest, if nothing else. Now, Jessica, get on with your tea; everyone else has finished. In fact, there's no need for any of you to wait for her."

Rosalind and Isabel and Sophie left the room. Jessica filled her mouth with bun. She realized that the lecture was not yet over. Her mother was waiting for the door to shut.

"Jessica, I did not want to say anything more in front of the others, but it really is too bad of you to be so careless. I am very cross indeed about this. Uncle Richard was looking for a job when he sent that money to you, and he's still looking for one. You must have heard Daddy and me talking about it."

Jessica swallowed her mouthful with difficulty.

"Why can't he get one, Mum?"

"He was a game-warden in Kenya. His qualifications don't fit him for anything over here."

"Couldn't he look after the lions at Whipsnade?"

"He's tried everything; he's tried the Zoo and Whipsnade. Now his money is running out and he can't afford a hotel any longer."

"Oh dear . . ."

"It *is* 'Oh dear', Jessica."

Jessica felt crushed indeed. She helped her mother clear away the tea, and then crept upstairs, meaning to push the offending postal order out of sight again. Her bedroom door stood open, and very clear, exquisitely enunciated words issued from it.

# *Arbutus Unedo*

*"Hamelin town's in Brunswick*
*By famous Hanover city.*
*The river Weser deep and wide*
*Washes its walls on the southern side.*
*A pleasanter spot you never spied.*
*But, when begins my ditty . . ."*

Jessica silently pushed the door further open. Sophie stood in front of the mirror, rounding her eyes at her own reflection, nodding her head and, actually, shaking a coy finger at her imaginary audience.

"Ditty", indeed. What a nauseating word! It just suited Sophie. Well, she wasn't going to fling herself on the bed with Sophie there, practising her piece in front of the mirror as if she were John Gielgud, she'd find somewhere else to recover. So she just darted to her chest-of-drawers, flung the postal order inside and rushed off again.

The drive at the bottom of the garden was the next best place.

When Rosalind had been less of a young lady and had enjoyed scrambling about, this had been a favourite place of theirs. It had led to a large old house called The Manor, but the house had been empty for some years and was due to be pulled down. The drive, in the meantime, had fallen into neglect. Moss and grass smothered the gravel path, and the bushes on either side, laurel and azalia and guelder rose, had grown tall and wild. A privet had grown up into a little tree and was now covered in its creamy-coloured flowers. Breaking into the fence of the next-door garden was the trunk of an oak tree. A low branch hung across their own part of the fence, and if you pulled yourself up on to the fence it acted as a kind of hand-rail. Jessica hoisted herself up, steadied herself with one hand on the branch, and then dropped down into the sunken depth of the drive below.

The ground level in the drive was about two feet below that of the garden. Jessica always enjoyed the sensation. She felt as if she were dropping into a hushed and secret world where it would be incongruous to make a noise. She stood quite still for a moment, enjoying the stillness. Then she noticed the little privet tree. She pulled down a branch and smelt the flowers. What a pity it was that their privet hedge was never given a chance to bloom.

"Jessica! Jessica!"

Jessica turned sharply round. Peering at her over the fence was Sophie. How ugly she looked, her face contorted in an effort to make herself heard.

"What do you want?"

"Mummy says you're to come in and do your homework at once!"

"Who told her I was out here?"

Sophie didn't mean to answer this question.

"You're to come at once," she reiterated.

"I'll come when I'm ready. I'm doing some Botany."

Sophie goggled and vanished.

Jessica returned her attention in a marked way to the privet. If observing a privet in its wild state wasn't Botany, she would like to know what was. But one couldn't exactly call it homework. Her homework that evening consisted of History and Arithmetic. But, no, wait! She had some Botany homework to do, even if it hadn't got to be done by tomorrow. Hadn't Miss Sims said, "I'm giving you two weeks, so that you will all have plenty of time in which to look around." They had been told to look for trees covering all the letters of the alphabet. But each bench had been given different letters. Jessica's bench had P to S. P for Privet: how fortunate!—unless Miss Sims, with her niggling insistence on accuracy, rejected privet on the grounds that it was a bush. There must be some tree in the avenue that would be a safer bet. Jessica looked hopefully around her. She wasn't fond of Botany, except when it gave her a chance to draw, and the sight of so many leaves suddenly overpowered her with boredom. For a second she stood there, half-inclined to give up all pretence of botanizing. Then her eyes fell on a tree she was quite certain was different from any she had ever seen before. Luckily she could just reach one dipping branch and wrench off a fair-sized bit.

Jessica, the twig between her teeth, climbed back over the fence into the garden. The french windows were open as she had left them, and she stepped through into the drawing-room on tiptoe, ears alert. Would her mother be impressed at her sudden interest in Botany or angry with her for not coming in at once?

Perhaps it would be just as well to be primed with information before she were caught.

The nature books were all in the bottom shelf of the bookcase in the drawing-room. Jessica plunged down on her knees, pulled out *Wayside and Woodland Trees* and started to leaf through it in a hurry.

She heard her mother's voice through the open door.

"Sophie dear, just run out again and see what Jessica's up to, will you?"

Footsteps approached. Jessica made herself small and held her breath. It was murky behind the sofa and there was every chance she wouldn't be seen. Motionless, she listened to the pad of Sophie's sandalled feet across the carpet and into the garden. Swiftly she returned to her book.

"Service, medlar, hawthorn . . ." It wasn't any of those. "Arbutus Unedo". That was a queer name. "Leaves, leathery, oval, two or three inches long, with toothed edges and hairy stalks." Just like her specimen! What a pity the name began with 'A'. But, wait, what was this? Strawberry Tree . . .

A shadow darkened the window. Sophie pattered across the carpet again, calling:

"Mummy, she's not there!"

It was time to brazen it out; make her presence known.

Jessica rose to her feet.

"I'm in *here*, Mum!"

"Where? Come into the dining-room at once!"

Jessica hesitated. She didn't want to be humiliated again in front of Isabel.

"Can't I do my Botany in here?"

"You heard what I said."

She'd have to go. Arming herself with unconcern, Jessica entered the dining-room. But although both Rosalind and Sophie were seated at the table with their books, there was no sign of Isabel. Oh, good. Jessica's confidence returned. Before her mother had time to open her mouth, she was pouring out a flood of information.

"Look, Mum, I've found an arbutus unedo. It's for our survey of trees in Westbridge. I found it in the drive, and it's quite rare, and it's nothing at all to do with a strawberry, it's ——"

"That will do, Jessica. Now just tell me why you didn't come in at once when I called?"

"Sophie said to come in and do my homework. Well, Botany is my homework and I was doing it."

Mrs. Rendell gave Jessica a very straight look.

"I didn't know you had Botany homework for Monday evenings."

"Well, not actually. You see, we're doing a survey —"

"You've told me that already. But you haven't told me when it's to be done by."

"Well, not for another two weeks actually, but Miss Sims told us to go about and keep our eyes open, and so ——"

"I see. Now sit down at once and get on with your proper homework. You've simply been wasting time."

"But, Mum, aren't you interested in my arbutus?"

"I shall be far more interested to see you getting on with what you're supposed to be doing. Put that twig away at once or I shall be extremely cross with you."

Jessica gave her mother a dark glance and pulled out her arithmetic book. Now if dear little Sophie had discovered the strawberry tree, there would have been cries of admiration at her being so clever. . . .

"Where's Isabel?"

"Get on with your *work*, Jessica."

The dining-room door opened softly. Isabel appeared with a book under her arm.

"Did you find what you wanted at the library, Isabel?"

"Yes, thank you, Aunt Lydia. I found *The Andes and the Amazon* by Orton."

"Oh dear, I think you'll find that a bit stiff."

Rosalind looked up. She spoke with warm-hearted enthusiasm.

"Mum, you've no idea how bright Isa is. Miss Kelly read out her essay to the whole class. She's keeping it to show the Head."

"Well done, Isabel." Mum sounded terribly pleased. "What was the subject of the essay?"

Jessica had stopped working at her sums and was following the whole conversation. She didn't think that Isabel was looking very pleased. She hesitated before replying, and then said:

" 'The Struggle for Existence in the Amazonian Forests.' "

"Geography is really your favourite subject?"

"Y-yes, I suppose it is."

Rosalind gave Isabel a bang on the back.

"She's absolutely top-notch at it, Mum. Last term Miss Kelly was saying that if only she could roll Clare and Susan Willis into one she'd have the perfect pupil, because Clare can always see what should go into an answer, and Susan can put it together properly. Now—lo and behold! like an answer to prayer, Isabel does both. Miss Kelly is thrilled: you can see she's planning a spectacular future for Isa. She says she can see the romance of the subject without just going woolly."

Jessica felt that far more enthusiasm was being shown to Isabel for her essay than had been evoked by her arbutus. And it wasn't as if Isabel was dying for praise. Far from it. She was looking thoroughly down-hearted.

"Mum, I know about the romance of places too.

> '*When I was but thirteen or so*
> *I went into a golden land:*
> *Chimborazo, Cotopaxi,*
> *Took me by the hand.*' "

Jessica managed to make the lines sound matter-of-fact.

"Well, that's jolly good news," said Rosalind. "Or—since you're only twelve—have we to wait two years for this happy event to take place?" She turned to Isabel. "Up till now, there've been just two poems she likes: 'I must arise and go now' and 'I must go down to the seas again', and we've been longing for her to decide which of the two impelling necessities would win."

This witty sally caused Sophie to collapse in giggles, and even Mrs. Rendell did not control an amused smile. But Isabel, Jessica noticed, only lowered her eyes to her book.

# 11

## *Uncle Richard*

Rosalind had succeeded in having her way. Uncle Richard was to have Isabel's room, and Isabel was to share with Rosalind. Isabel quite took it for granted that she would be sleeping on the camp bed which had been brought up from under the stairs, but Rosalind simply wouldn't hear of it.

"Isa, you are to have my bed. I insist! I adore camp beds: they go down so snugly in the middle. Oh, Mum," cried Rosalind, turning to her mother and seizing her round the waist, "won't it be fun! Isa and I will be talking away all night!"

It was Saturday morning. Mrs. Rendell and Rosalind were helping Isabel to move her belongings, while Jessica hung about watching.

"I hope you won't, Rosalind," said Mrs. Rendell. "In fact, I shall be very cross if you keep Isabel awake with your chatter. You have all day to talk in."

"Rosalind had the whole of school time to talk to Clare. Yet she used to ring her up every single evening and talk some more," pointed out Jessica.

"Jessica, instead of standing and talking yourself, perhaps you would help," said Mrs. Rendell.

Isabel, defeated over the camp bed, was silently engaged in emptying her wardrobe. Jessica went to help her; and Mrs. Rendell said:

"Isabel dear, I don't think there'll be room for everything in Rosalind's wardrobe. I'll find you some room in mine."

"My winter things could be packed away in my trunk," said Isabel. "They will only be in your way."

"Oh, nonsense! It isn't as if Uncle Richard is going to stop for ever."

"While Isa is with us for keeps!" cried Rosalind warmly. She seized the winter coat which Jessica was clutching and rushed off with it to her mother's room.

"Rosalind ——" began Mrs. Rendell. She had followed Rosalind across the landing, and now lowered her voice before she went on speaking. ". . . you heard what I said about the night-time? Isabel has been looking very strained lately."

"Mum, she works too hard at her lessons. I'm always telling her off about it."

"Well, please don't keep her awake." The sight of Jessica, all ears at the door, reminded her mother of something else. "And aren't you neglecting Clare a little these days?"

"No, Mum, I'm not. She's neglecting me! She's behaving most peculiarly. I think she's jealous of Isabel."

"You may have given her some cause."

"I've been as nice as sugar to her. But she just won't make a threesome. It's pure selfishness wanting me all to herself."

"Hush! don't let Isabel . . ."

Jessica vanished and reappeared again in Uncle Richard's room. It was looking very bare, but still smelt faintly of Isabel's talcum powder. Isabel herself was standing in front of the dressing-table mirror, very slowly drawing her comb through her blonde hair. Indeed, her movement was so soft and gentle that Jessica guessed beyond any doubt that she must have overheard every word. . . .

Uncle Richard was supposed to arrive in time for tea on Tuesday. When Jessica woke on that morning she realized at once that she had something nice to look forward to. Neither her estrangement from Nance nor her fear of Syd Bulsher would weigh so heavy on her spirit today. Her joy, alas, could not be unalloyed because of the postal order. If her uncle looked poverty-stricken she would feel constantly reproached. She had made various attempts to find out from her mother exactly how poor he was; but the reply, "I'm not saying he's *completely* penniless, Jessica," left just about everything to the imagination.

At the end of the afternoon she could see Syd hanging about near the door as she came out of school. Although he was only thirteen he was huge; and he stood there with his great thumbs tucked into his wide black leather belt and his bored eyes flicking over the crowd as they came tumbling down the steps on to the asphalt. Had she seen a spark come into those eyes as they fell on her? Jessica's heart pounded and her cheeks reddened. It was impossible to disguise her fear by an air of unconcern; Syd *knew* that her heart was pounding. Somehow or other she had to get past him quickly; she wanted to get home intact and without delay. She tried to keep her eyes off his pointed shoes; she would never forget the time Syd had suddenly stuck out a foot and sent Jessica sprawling, her knees grazed and bleeding, her hands pitted with the gravel, while Bunny just stood there nervously giggling. Even his own family were scared of Syd. He was an *awful* boy, far worse than Charlie McQueen, who had once frightened Jessica into fits by pretending to be a mad dog and snarling and yapping and biting at her heels as he followed her up a deserted staircase one day. Syd would never do anything at the same time funny and frightening like that.

She was almost up to him when there came a sweet and unexpected deliverance. That new boy from Wales whose gentle sing-song voice Syd had been heard ridiculing as "soft" in the playground yesterday had accosted him. Caught unawares, Syd had squared up to him and at once the two were engaged in a furious fight. Jessica slid past them, took to her heels, and ran.

The kitchen smelt deliciously of baking, but it was empty. The whole place was quiet. Yet Jessica could sense a new presence in the house. She walked through into the hall, and then saw, through the open dining-room door, a tall figure standing in front of the window and gazing out. He looked lonely. Jessica forgot about the postal order.

"Hullo, Uncle."

Uncle Richard swung round in a flash. He might have been in Africa, not Westbridge. But when he saw who it was, he smiled.

"Jessica! Hullo . . ."

They shook hands. Jessica gazed up at him with admiration. He was very good-looking and very shy, and this made a fascinating combination. She could see him desperately racking his brains for something to say.

"Just back from school?"

Jessica agreed that she was.

"Er . . . like it?"

"It's all right."

Uncle Richard nervously stirred the hair on the back of his head. But at that instant Mrs. Rendell came into the room, followed almost immediately by Rosalind, Sophie and Isabel. Uncle Richard looked shyer than ever, but what with Isabel being introduced to him, and Rosalind talking sixteen to the dozen, and Sophie holding up her face to be kissed, he did not need to say very much. And then Sophie created a diversion by dismissing him entirely and turning all her attention on her mother.

"Mummy! Mummy! You know I'm reciting 'The Pied Piper' at the Garden Party?"

"Yes, darling, I do. I'm looking forward to it. Now, all of you, run upstairs and tidy yourselves, and then we'll have tea!"

"Mummy ——" Sophie pressed a white envelope on her mother. "This is the invitation!"

"*Thank* you, darling! Now run along, quickly."

"Come on, Sophie!" said Jessica sharply.

Sophie could always convey the impression that she was obeying nobody but herself. She brushed her hair neatly, washed her hands without leaving any grime on the towel, and was back downstairs in a flash to watch her mother draw the invitation from the envelope.

Uncle Richard was so tongue-tied during tea that perhaps it was just as well that Sophie made herself the focus of attention. Jessica noticed her uncle devour a scone in two bites, and then bashfully realize his empty plate. Silently she pushed the dish towards him again, while Mrs. Rendell read out the invitation for all to hear and Sophie sat bathed in self-importance, her eyes fixed on her mother's face.

The Misses Fanshawe and Staff<br>have great pleasure<br>in inviting<br>Mr. and Mrs. Rendell<br>to a garden party and entertainment<br>in the School Grounds<br>on Saturday July 15th<br>at 3 p.m.

"Darling," said Mrs. Rendell, "it sounds lovely. I'll write and accept this evening."

"Mummy, I'm the chief person in 'The Pied Piper'. I recite it while the others act the mime."

"Couldn't we all cram in and see it?" said Rosalind. "I'd love to see the infants togged up as rats eating the other infants in their cradles."

"Miss Fanshawe says if we've got sisters who are 'old girls' she'll be glad of their help with the refreshments."

"Count me out," said Jessica quickly. "I'd only spill the tea, and I'm sick to death of 'The Pied Piper' already."

"Jessica, that's very rude. And even if you think you're tired of hearing Sophie, Miss Fanshawe is a brilliant producer, and I'd be very sorry to miss the entertainment."

Mortified, Jessica hunched her shoulders and glanced up under her lashes at Uncle Richard. He had chopped a slice of cake into little bits and was trying to eat it slowly.

"Uncle Richard ——" Sophie turned towards her uncle, all big hazel eyes, and put a hand on his sleeve—"would *you* like to hear me recite the poem?"

Everybody watched. Uncle Richard was looking at Sophie as if she was much too fragile and alarming to be within fifty yards of him.

"Of course," he managed to mutter.

"After tea?"

"Darling," interrupted her mother, "you really shouldn't worry your uncle on his very first evening."

"Why not?"

"He may be tired."

Tired? . . . But one couldn't ever imagine Uncle Richard being tired. He moved in a springy, caged sort of way like a tiger needing more exercise. Bored, restless? That was another matter. Jessica, in the ten days which followed, would often see him standing in front of the dining-room window, jingling coins in his pocket, staring out. It was, of course, reassuring to hear that he had coins to jingle, reassuring to note that his grey flannels and his tweed jacket, with the white V of a handkerchief showing in the pocket, showed no signs of being threadbare: poverty couldn't be the main problem. No, the problem was having nothing to do. Mother had a hundred and one things with which to fill her day, apart from all the fussing; Uncle Richard had exactly one. Instead of Father, he took Sophie across the dangerous crossing on

her way to school. Jessica would watch Sophie's legs go twinkle, twinkle beside Uncle Richard's long, easy stride. But then what? "Anything you want down-town, Lydia?" she had heard him ask her mother one morning. Mother racked her brains to think of jobs for him, but she was not the sort of person who was always longing for an electrician or a plumber or a carpenter; her mind was always on her next committee meeting. Jessica suggested he cut a little eight-inch door in the garage, so that Claudius, who liked to be out at night, could squeeze into the garage when it rained, but the idea received no support from her parents. It seemed as if all the practical possibilities had been exhausted: he had cleaned out the garage, re-organized the tool-shed, put a new washer on a tap, and addressed some envelopes for her mother. Now he was left with empty hours stretching before him, when he wandered from room to room, from window to window, staring out with his sailor's eyes. Sometimes, when she came in from school, he would be dozing in a deck-chair in the garden and Jessica would be sent out to tell him tea was ready. He always sprang up at once, alert, nervous and very shy. "Ah, Jessica! tea ready?" he would say energetically, as if this was the beginning of some brilliant conversational gambit. But that was as far as it went.

If only he wasn't so shy of everybody. It seemed so odd to be scared of nothing but quite harmless things. Jessica felt that he would have welcomed with gratitude and relief a man-eating tiger or an armed gangster. But what hope was there of an encounter with either of these in Westbridge?

# 12

## *The Strawberry Tree*

Jessica stood at the dining-room window, slowly licking a marmalade spoon and watching Uncle Richard and Sophie cross the road hand in hand and disappear round the corner. She was just about to turn away when someone else came into immediate view. It was Bunny Bulsher, his big ears and his round eyes showing above the privet hedge.

Jessica leaned out of the open, summery window.

"I'm not ready yet. You can come in and clear the breakfast things, if you like."

Bunny was the most amenable boy imaginable; as different from his brother as chalk from cheese. He did not in the least resent Jessica's rather cavalier treatment of him or the fact that she only put up with his company to school in order to avoid the embarrassment of running straight into Nance. He came in at once, wiping his clean shoes on the mat.

Luckily her mother was busy phoning. She only gave a surprised stare when Bunny emerged from the dining-room carrying a load of breakfast things. But when

Jessica rushed out at her, crying, "Someone has thrown away my arbutus!" she put her hand over the phone, and said, shortly:

"Nobody has touched it, Jessica. It is where you left it last night in the kitchen."

Yes, this was the great day: the day when Jessica would stand up in Botany class and surprise everybody with her discovery.

It was a bit dashing to find that Bunny didn't even want to take a peep into her cone of paper. But that was the snag about Bunny: apart from food, there was only one thing in which he was interested—aeroplanes. Jessica had thought that being a boy he would be sure to show some excitement when she told him about Uncle Richard and his work as a game-warden in Africa. Bunny had, indeed, appeared to be listening, but then, suddenly, he had yelled out, "A Comet can go from here to Nairobi in twelve hours; like this ——" And then he had stuck out his arms and rushed zooming ahead, looking like a lunatic. So she should have been prepared for his complete indifference to her arbutus.

But suppose nobody was going to be interested. . . .

Botany was the last lesson of a very sultry afternoon. The windows were all wide open, but not a breath of air came in, only the hot roar of the motor-mower approaching, turning, and receding with sickening regularity. Jessica's bare arms stuck to the bench as if they were in contact with lukewarm gum; her cotton frock stuck to her chest. She took a swift glance round her. Certainly she need not fear competition, for she could see that the rest of the form were in the last stages of ennui. They all sprawled at the benches with their legs stuck out askew, puffing out their cheeks and scowling. The entrance of Miss Sims caused a momentary diversion. She had actually discarded her drooping grey cardigan, disclosing a short-sleeved blouse underneath. Her pale, match-stick arms made everyone stare; their own were so brown.

"Miss Sims!" Nance had sprung to her feet. And now everyone stared at Nance from their lounging positions; she sounded extraordinarily determined. Where did she find the energy?

"Miss Sims—it's stifling in here. Couldn't we have our lesson outside under the trees?"

It took poor Miss Sims a moment or two to quell the uproar that followed, and then another few minutes to make it quite clear that the suggestion was strictly against the rules. But this did not satisfy Nance. She remained completely detached from the clamour, waiting silent on her feet until she could again command the whole of Miss Sims's attention.

"Miss Sims, I can quite see how Mr. Stephens feels about *other* lessons held out of doors. But Botany *belongs* out of doors. We should have examples of trees all around us. *And* ——"

"You heard what I have just said to the class. Sit down, Nance, and let us get on with our lesson."

But Nance wouldn't sit down. Perhaps the heat had got under her skin and made her more argumentative than usual. It was not like her to disregard Miss Sims's expression of suffering; nor, indeed, was it like her to be unaware that Jessica was gazing at her with reproach and dismay.

"Miss Sims, you *must* listen. It isn't the actual temperature in here I can't stand. It's the muck sweat we're all in. Not to mention the din that old mower makes."

"All right, Nance . . ." Miss Sims stood there, quiet, long-suffering, dogged, but clearly near the end of her tether. Faces which had split into grins again during Nance's last harangue suddenly straightened. Miss Sims did look bad. ". . . if you would rather spend my lessons outside this door where you will find the air a little less oppressive, you may do so. But kindly go at once if you are going . . ."

Nance shot down on to her stool with a bang. Expressionless, she glanced at nobody.

". . . then we'll begin," said Miss Sims. Jessica, clasping her twig hopefully in front of her, was aware that Miss Sims was making an enormous effort to pull herself together, to be lively, and interesting. ". . . now we've all been busy during the last two weeks keeping our eyes open and making a study of our local trees. Well, the very first thing we must do is to appoint a secretary who will jot down our findings. Later, we shall use these notes to make a valuable book of reference for the library. Now, who would like to be our scribe?"

Of all the soft ideas! Thirty blank pairs of eyes stared back at Miss Sims. Nobody? Then Derrick Byrne was heard to mutter that he didn't mind if he did, his big sister was learning shorthand.

"Splendid, Derrick. Write down the name of the tree, its habitat, and the name of the person who found it, so that we can refer for details later. Then we'll start right away with our findings. Row A to E at the front. Caroline, you stand up first and let us hear what you've found."

Jessica grasped her twig tighter than ever; her eyes grew large. Anyone in row A to E might forestall her and her lovely tree would be worthless. Wasn't its botanical name "arbutus" just as correct as its other name "strawberry tree"?—indeed, more so. But Caroline had discovered nothing other than beech and chestnut trees in the park. And so had Peter, Jo, Howard, Jim and Daphne. Jo had also found an acorn tree and was told that an oak tree wouldn't count under that name. Jessica ran her tongue nervously round her mouth. How shattering if 'strawberry' didn't count either.

Miss Sims was looking pained. Had nobody found a cedar tree or an elder tree? Had nobody got an apple tree in their back garden?

Nobody. The faces in the front row wore the secretive expression of those who have done absolutely no work and mean to lie as low as possible.

"Well, let us go on and see if row F to I have used their eyes to better advantage."

Row F to I had discovered horse-chestnut trees in the school grounds.

Two red spots appeared in Miss Sims's cheeks and suffused the hollows above her jaw-bones.

Janice, Chloe, Ray and Bertram in row J to O had spotted both lime trees and may trees in the park. They were vociferous in pointing out to Miss Sims that the red and white may trees were planted round the ice-cream parlour. But Madeline and Rupert had really done their homework. They had set out on their bicycles on Sunday afternoon and had seen an oak (holm), a Judas Tree, laburnum, mulberry, Mountain Ash, European Larch, Norway Maple and osier.

"Miss Sims, I can't take down all that jaw," said Derrick sulkily.

"Rupert and Madeline, I see, have made their own notes," said Miss Sims, in commending tones. She asked Madeline to explain to the class the difference between a holm oak and the common oak, *Quercus robur*.

Madeline was a shy, model little girl. She did as she was told, and the class gaped at her and then lapsed back into boredom. Two inky pellets flipped across the laboratory, plopping down on to a bench like dragonflies over a stagnant pond. "Nobody will listen to me when it's my turn," thought Jessica, in an agony.

Miss Sims was a fraction too late spotting the origin of the pellets. She stared; the children stared back.

"If you would all sit up properly, you would feel a great deal more alert. You are not helping yourselves.... That's better. Now the next row, P to S." Miss Sims hesitated just a second. "Nance..."

Miss Sims had started at the right-hand end of Jessica's row, instead of the left. Perhaps she wished to get Nance over and done with before her patience gave out. Jessica's place was second from the left end. It was frustrating having to wait even longer than she had anticipated.

But apparently Nance had been waiting with as much eagerness as Jessica. Once again she had shot to her feet.

"Miss Sims, there's a poplar at the bottom of our garden. I don't care what sort, but it shouldn't be there.

My Dad's been on and on to the Council about it, but——"

The class brightened like magic. Nance had her audience whether she cared tuppence for it or not.

"Now that's enough, Nance, you're wandering away from the point. Is that the only tree you've found? You didn't look very far, did you, if you looked no further than your back garden?"

"Miss Sims, I'm coming to the point. The point is that poplars shouldn't be close to houses. The roots get into the foundations. Dad says if the Council don't do something soon the whole box of tricks will come down on our heads one day."

"It is quite true what you say, Nance; poplar trees should be at least fifty yards from a building. But your father's complaints to the Council have absolutely nothing to do with my lesson. Now, please sit down."

The class watched Nance as she slumped down on her stool again, muttering. But if Nance was indifferent to their attention, Jessica was not. This was the moment to seize.

"Miss Sims, could *I* be next?"

Miss Sims drew in her chin. Enthusiasm, on the rare occasions she came across it, was always spoilt by insubordination.

"I wonder why you can't wait your turn, Jessica, like everybody else? William . . .?"

Bunny got to his feet and said that he had seen a sycamore tree in the park.

Miss Sims gazed for a long sad moment at Bunny. Then she said:

"There are no sycamore trees in the park, William."

This declaration, uttered very gravely, cast the fidgeting children into a sudden, uneasy silence. Miss Sims looked so old, so grey, so *disappointed*.

"It appears to me," she said, "that not one of you, with the exception of Madeline and Rupert, has taken the trouble to observe any trees at all. All you have done is to blandly assume that any tree you have heard of beginning with your letters of the alphabet can be found in the park. That is all the effort you have made."

Miss Sims paused and allowed her words to sink in. She was good at long, reproachful silences. One or two of the more susceptible in the class hung their heads. But not Jessica.

"Miss Sims, you haven't asked *me* yet!"

Miss Sims met this challenge with another silent look. She had always found Jessica one of her most troublesome pupils. True, she could draw botanical specimens very prettily, but in class her head was always screwed round in conversation with someone.

"Very well, Jessica, you may have your turn now."

Now that her chance had come, Jessica could hardly get her words out. "My tree—what I found—it's a strawberry."

The effect was overwhelming.

"Cor, Jess, did you pick some?"

"Show us, Jess!"

"I bet she's eaten 'em all herself. Haven't you, Greedy!"

"Quietly, everybody!" cried Miss Sims.

"Miss Sims," Jessica looked a little ruffled, "it's a strawberry *tree*—an arbutus."

"Yah! an arbutus is a little old kind of gun. Says so in my comic this week."

Miss Sims restored order, and then turned to Ray Taylor.

"You're confusing 'arbutus' with 'arquebus'—a word of an entirely different derivation."

Ray did not like his mistake being given such weighty condemnation. He looked sulky. Miss Sims turned back to Jessica.

"This is most interesting, Jessica. Tell us all where you found it. Now, listen, everybody."

"In the avenue at the end of our garden, Miss Sims."

"Ah, I imagined it would be in cultivated ground. I suppose, as it's so close to your own garden, you have permission to trespass?"

"I don't feel I'm trespassing, Miss Sims. The Manor has been empty for ages."

"The Manor! Coo! that's where they found somebody's head in a suitcase!"

"You're bats!" cried Nance. "That's the Manor over by Dyke's Cross. Jessica means a house back of Maytree Avenue."

"Quiet, everybody," said Miss Sims.

" 'Tis so, Miss Sims," pressed Howard. "It's where the murder was two years back. They found the woman's head in a trunk. I ought to know, my Dad's a policeman."

"But it's not that Manor we're talking about, you gump!" retorted Nance. "Go on, Jess. You tell 'im."

But neither Jessica nor Miss Sims herself had a chance for the next minute. Most of the class had vague memories of the murder, and correspondingly exact views as to where it had taken place; those who remembered nothing were avid to learn. The laboratory was suddenly alive with argument and exposition.

Had it not been so hot, and had she not been aware that the bell would very shortly bring an end to the lesson, Miss Sims would perhaps not have pretended to herself that the sudden explosion of interest could be converted to botanical purposes. Perhaps, too, her pleasure at one genuine find in an afternoon of disappointments caused her judgement to falter.

"Quiet, all of you. Jessica has already told us where the tree is. I'm glad to see so many of you interested. I should certainly like to see it myself; the strawberry tree is not common at all. What about it, Jessica? Do you think there would be any harm in anyone who's interested going up the avenue to look at it?"

This was most gratifying. Miss Sims really did look pleased. Grateful to her for bringing the class back to her discovery, Jessica responded with enthusiasm: "I don't see why not, Miss Sims, there's no one to stop them. The avenue is just round the corner in Sinclair Road, and the gate is always open. Actually, it's fallen off its hinge and got stuck in the gravel."

Miss Sims just had time before the bell rang to say she would be at the top of the avenue at three o'clock on Saturday afternoon, and anyone who would like to examine the tree with her was to meet her there.

# 13

## *The Riot*

The next day a prefect came up to Jessica in the dinner-hour and told her that Miss Sims wished to speak to her and that she would find her in the "big" staff-room.

As Jessica mounted the stairs she heard a great deal of laughter coming from the "big" staff-room, and it struck her as a strange place for Miss Sims, who always looked so subdued. She was just about to knock when Miss Sims herself opened the door, letting out a great blast of noise and tobacco smoke. She was back in her drooping grey cardigan. Swiftly and quietly she closed the door behind her.

"Oh, Jessica," she said, "I'm so sorry, but I shan't be able to see your tree tomorrow. The fact is ——" and here Miss Sims made a great effort to lift her voice to a bright note—"my mother is not at all well—not at all, actually—and I don't like to leave her."

Jessica was astonished to learn that old Miss Sims had a mother.

"Oh . . . Oh, I am sorry, Miss Sims."

"It's just one of those things one must expect. She's a good age, you know." Miss Sims looked down at Jessica with mild pride. "Ninety."

The old lady was going to die beyond a doubt. Jessica was aghast; but she said earnestly: "I do hope she'll soon be better, Miss Sims."

"Oh, I'm sure she'll be her old self in a day or two. I put it down to the heat. But I really don't think I ought to leave her . . ." Worry frayed Miss Sims's face again; she could not sound confident for long. "So if you'd just explain, and be there yourself in case . . . I think it most unlikely that anyone will turn up but Madeline and Rupert, now that they realize ——" and here Miss Sims gave her small smile—"that there really are no strawberries on strawberry trees."

"I'll tell them."

"If you will, Jessica."

Miss Sims disappeared into the alien noise again, and Jessica returned with slow steps to the playground. She knew that she was usually a great trial to Miss Sims because she was "always talking" and "inattentive"; but now there had been a change in their relationship. With her back against the shut door of the staff-room Miss Sims had talked to her as if she were the one attentive person in the whole world.

The dinner-hour was still going on. Jessica stood by herself, staring with vacant eyes at the shouting groups of boys and girls that moved like a kaleidoscope before her vision. She was picturing Miss Sims in a different rôle from that of a teacher of Botany. Miss Sims filling hot-water bottles, carrying up trays. It was a long way from

"Now, Jessica, look what you're doing with that apparatus, please . . ."

The bell rang. Jessica stepped backwards to save herself being knocked over by a rush of children bearing down in her direction. What was that other remark Miss Sims had let fall? "But if you'd just be there . . ."

Only then did it strike Jessica that she had been virtually left in charge. If no one but Madeline and Rupert was going to turn up, her rôle would amount to nothing. They were both so very well-behaved. But suppose others less well-behaved took it into their heads to come. Who knows, they might consider it a tremendous lark to run wild over a private property where there was nobody about to say them nay. For there it all was, the avenue, the copse, the garden, the empty house, a whole unexplored terrain, secret until she had stood up in the class and revealed its whereabouts. And if they did all come, what would she be able to do but stand helpless as they rushed and shouted and trampled their way everywhere. . . .

Jostled and elbowed out of her dream again, Jessica allowed herself to be pushed along, almost without volition on her part, in at the playground door, along a corridor thunderous with feet, to the very door of her class-room; a daily hazard, made just endurable by the restraining influence of a prefect on duty. It was a frightening foretaste of what barbarian hordes might do when there was no authority about at all. Dazed, Jessica sank down in her desk. Of course she should tell the class *now* that the whole thing was off for Saturday afternoon, tell them that nobody was to turn up. But might not that be the very way to make them all come in a body? Perhaps the quieter she kept about it, the better. She wished that she could unburden herself to someone. Nance was the very person, only she was not on speaking terms with her. Jessica swivelled round in her desk. Bunny's big ears caught the light from the window. He was drawing an aeroplane and looked at peace with the world.

"Miss Sims's mother is ill. She can't come to see my tree on Saturday. I don't want anyone to come and see it."

Bunny looked up. He stared with open mouth at Jessica's face scowling anxiously into his.

"What tree?"

"You know . . . my strawberry tree."

Bunny brightened.

"Where they found that suitcase with the head in it?"

Mr. Tomkins had entered with his forceful air. Everyone was standing up.

"No!" hissed Jessica, crimson-faced, "*not* where they found it."

Really, Bunny was the stupidest boy.

On Saturday morning there were purple clouds massing behind the houses opposite, and bursts of sunlight.

"Oh, don't let it rain!" cried Rosalind. She had come down to breakfast looking very clean in a white blouse and shorts. "We must play our match against Burchester High!"

"Mum," said Sophie, laying a finger on her mother's sleeve, "don't let it rain *next* Saturday. It's our Garden Party."

"Let it rain and rain," intoned Jessica. "Let the heavens be opened!"

Everybody stared at Jessica.

"Mother," exclaimed Rosalind, in indignant and almost frightened tones, "whatever is she doing? Stop it, Jessica!"

"Jessica is only being silly," said Mrs. Rendell, after meeting an inscrutable look from under her daughter's fringe. "Isabel, what sort of day are you hoping for?"

"Isa wants it fine!" said Rosalind eagerly. "She is coming to cheer me on."

"I said, if you didn't mind, I wouldn't," said Isabel. "I did tell you I wanted to get on with my Biology, and then buy that present for Maimie's birthday."

"But I was going to help you choose! I love looking for presents."

"Rosalind," said her mother, "you must let Isabel do some things on her own."

"Why, yes, if she wants to," said Rosalind, in puzzled, but good-natured tones.

The rain did hold off all the morning. Rosalind went off to play in her match, and Isabel worked at her prep. until half-past eleven; then she disappeared. Jessica stood at the window looking out in rather the same way that Uncle Richard would stand and look out. But she was feeling nervous, not bored.

If only it would rain, then *nobody* would turn up.

Rosalind returned from her match, victorious; Isabel came back from shopping. As the family sat at lunch, huge spots like florins hit the paving stones below the window.

"There is your rain, Jessica," said her mother.

But no sooner had she spoken than there was silence again. The thunder spots evaporated as if they had never been. Jessica's mouth went dry too.

At three o'clock Jessica made her way down the garden, pulled herself to the top of the fence, and then dropped, down, down, into the sunken avenue below.

A bird plunged out of a nearby bush, frightened.

It was dead quiet in the avenue now that the bird had gone. In the silence one could hear the cars roaring up the hill beyond the gates. And how dark and sultry the air was under the trees!

Jessica ran on tiptoe along the mossy path until she came to her strawberry tree. The grey trunk stood out against the thicket beyond. Above her head the little dark leaves almost shut out the sky.

Something small—a mouse?—darted out from the bushes.

Jessica nearly jumped out of her skin. Then she felt annoyed at this display of fright. She wasn't afraid of mice; she'd see if there was another, perhaps a family of baby mice. She crouched down, her nose close to the bushes, and peered in through the tangle of brushwood.

There was something there. A large inanimate object. It looked like an old . . .

It *was* an old suitcase.

Jessica scrambled quickly away from it. Then, still on her haunches, she peered again, hypnotized. Howard and Ralph and Bunny had all been so sure . . . And now here was another suitcase, battered, grimy, concealing its horrible and gory contents. . . .

"Jessica! Jess! Coo-eee!"

Three small figures had appeared at the road end of the avenue. They had seen her and were waving and shouting.

"Are there no others? Is it just you?" she asked eagerly, as they met.

"It looks like it," said Rupert. He stared about him, taking in the silence of the avenue.

"It's sort of spooky in here," said Madeline.

"It's the birds. They go quiet before a storm," said Jessica. She looked at Bunny. "I do hope no one else is coming."

Bunny thrust his hands in his pockets, grinned sheepishly and wriggled his behind.

"Where's the tree?" said Rupert. He pushed his spectacles up and took out a note-book and pencil.

"Over here," said Jessica. She led the way up to it, and then tipped her head backwards, directing their eyes upwards into the umbrella of leaves. If Bunny noticed the suitcase, he would immediately suppose it to contain a severed head. His belief would infect them all. They would all draw back from it, staring with round-eyed horror. Far better to pretend it wasn't there.

But Rupert had stopped gazing upwards and was now examining the trunk with a scientific eye.

"I should come away, if I were you," said Jessica. "You could be struck by lightning."

"Haven't you anything to tell us about the tree?" asked Madeline. "I wish Miss Sims was here."

"No, I haven't. And I think we ought to go before the storm breaks."

"Oh, Jess," said Bunny, in a small voice, "it's too late."

Jessica did not have to ask what he meant. A rabble of

children had turned into the avenue from the road and were advancing towards them. The boys scuffled and fought among themselves, while the girls—there were only two of them—walked arm-in-arm, shouting repartee at the boys, but keeping a safe distance. As they drew nearer to the four waiting children, the fighting stopped. Jessica could see that their attention was now entirely fixed on her; and with a sinking heart she saw just who they were. There was no mistaking Syd and his gang. How slowly and silently they advanced towards her. . . .

Syd hitched up his trousers and came and stood squarely in front of her. Jessica was suddenly able to move. She took a step backwards and stumbled against the roots of her tree. The jolt made her look extra frightened.

"Well, where's this flipping tree of yours?"

"Here."

Anything to direct attention from herself. In a moment she would point out the gory suitcase. . . .

"I don't see no flipping strawberries on it."

"It doesn't have strawberries on it, Syd."

"Then you're a liar. What you got us all down here for? Come on now—out with it! And, look ——" Syd suddenly shot forward his neck, so that his face with its puffy lips was only a few inches from Jessica's—"don't you go running with no tales about me to that Nance. Or I'll cut both yer throats."

"Running with tales? . . ." Jessica felt for the tree trunk behind her. She pressed her back against it. "What tales?"

"*You* know."

"I don't . . . I don't . . ."

"Come off it, Syd," said a voice. "It's the house we've

come to see, not the tree or the kid. Now, Miss Rendell . . ."

It was Charlie speaking to her. He had elbowed Syd to one side, and was now standing in front of her, taking a pencil from behind his ear. "I am Inspector McQueen and this is my colleague, Sergeant Bulsher. If you would just give us the facts of the murder ——"

Jessica looked straight into Charlie's merry, mock-solemn eyes.

"Honest, Charlie, it isn't this house."

"I understand that this avenue leads us to The Manor?"

"Yes . . . yes, but it's not the one you mean!"

"Miss Rendell, I must warn you it's a serious matter to try and give a false testimony to the police."

"I'm not giving a false testimony. You know it's not this Manor."

Syd thrust his way between them.

"Look, the strawberry tree ain't a strawberry tree and the blooming Manor ain't the Manor. Her brains want examining. Let's take a look at 'em."

Syd seized Jessica's arm and jerked her roughly towards him. Jessica shrieked.

"Shut your mouth. Sneak. Cry-baby." He twisted her arm behind her and was forcing her to her knees.

"Don't," said Jessica, in a small, smothered voice, "don't."

"Oh, pack it up, Syd," said Charlie. "The kid's frightened."

"She's a custard all right. I'll show 'er. And you keep your mouth shut too."

Nobody was going to help her now. The boys just

stood; the girls gaped. The avenue was dead quiet. Then suddenly, loud as pistol shots, hail fell from the sky.

It was so sudden that even Syd let go of Jessica to gape for a second upward.

"This way!" cried Charlie.

They all began to run in the same direction, the boys ducking their heads, the girls screaming and trying to protect their faces from the stinging, bouncing balls of hail. Breathless they reached the house with its wide verandah and huddled against the walls. Above their heads the hail hit the glass with a deafening crack and then slid down to the gravel. Benumbed by the noise, the children stared out. The downpour obscured the garden in a silver veil. . . .

Then someone said, in surprised tones: "It's stopped!"

The roar had ceased. The garden became vivid again.

They trooped out from under the verandah. The hail still lay like camphor balls, but already the sun was drawing a steamy heat from the earth and there was a hot-house smell everywhere. Overhead the sky was a bright blue.

For another moment the transformation was a matter for wonder. Then everybody turned their attention on the house. They stepped back and gazed up at it. To Jessica the sight was familiar enough: the flat, slate roof, the long row of the upper windows with their faded shutters, the ground-floor ones half-hidden by tangled sprays of clematis and roses which covered the roof of the verandah and hung down in festoons. The front door, with its columned porch, looked as if no one had used its knocker for a long time. Jessica had observed months ago how the grass had seeded itself in the mat which lay on the wide, shallow step. How utterly shut up and deserted the whole house looked! Yet what was Syd doing? He had tried the handle of the conservatory at the end and now had his shoulder against the door. Push . . . Push . . . The door shuddered and opened.

It was only a small green-house, and there was nothing inside but cracked seed-boxes and plants so old and dried-up that they crumbled at a touch; and a tank full of dark, brackish water.

Yet everyone crowded inside except Jessica and Bunny and Rupert and Madeline.

"Ought they to go in?" said Rupert to Jessica.

Jessica took a deep breath and said nothing.

Syd was now trying the door on the other side of the green-house, throwing his weight against that. For a moment or two it trembled and shuddered, resisting his efforts. Then he gave a third, violent heave, the door gave, and he was through.

His friends followed him. The darkness of the room swallowed them up.

At first it seemed as if they were overawed by the silence, for Jessica, watching their disappearance inside, heard nothing. Then, gradually, thumps and bumps could be heard, bursts of laughter, the thunder of feet up uncarpeted stairs.

"I think we'll go home," said Madeline to Rupert.

Without a word to Jessica they turned and walked away.

Jessica realized that their presence was no help to her, yet the way they coolly detached themselves from the

situation and walked off, was too much for her feelings. She rounded on Bunny.

"It's all your fault!"

Bunny shuffled his feet.

"I didn't know Syd would turn up. All I did was to tell Mum about your old strawberry tree. Syd ain't never been interested in trees before. I didn't even know he was listening."

"You're just daft. I never tell them anything at home."

"Don't you think *we*'d better clear off?"

"No, I don't. And don't you dare leave me. I'm in charge here."

Poor Bunny had one thing to commend him. He never criticized or answered back. Anyone else in his shoes would have retorted, "If you're in charge, *do* something," but Bunny only squirmed and tried to evade Jessica's scowling eye by gazing vacantly around him.

At that instant Jessica's attention was drawn back to the house by the sudden appearance of Charlie on a balcony. He had thrown open a french window on the first floor, and was now leaning over the iron fretwork of the balcony, his arms flung wide.

" 'Friends, Romans, countrymen, lend me your ears ——' "

He got no further. Four boys sprang on him from behind, and dragged him backwards through the french window. Charlie kicked out. His shoe crashed through glass. The french window clashed to behind them, dislodging a splinter of glass which shattered itself on the balcony.

Jessica put her hands over her ears.

"I can't stand any more. We'll have to go home."

"Come on," said Bunny.

But Jessica was still staring up at the house as if incapable of moving. Bunny seized her hand and pulled her round.

Then they saw Nance. She had just that instant appeared round the curve of the avenue and was hurrying towards them.

Jessica gave a little cry, snatched her hand from Bunny's and ran the few yards to meet her.

"I couldn't come any sooner," Nance panted. "Mum wanted me to help her cut out a blouse, and then the hail came down like billy-o . . . Hullo ——" she blew a strand of hair from her face and glanced up at the house. "What's going on in there?"

"Oh, Nance, it's Syd and that lot. They're breaking everything up!"

"Sounds like it," said Nance. She stared up at the house as another crash resounded. "We'll have to get 'em out of there somehow. Jess, is yer Dad at home?"

"Yes—I mean, no. This is his Saturday for being on call," said Jessica, instantly flustered.

"Well, you go along in and see. It wouldn't take him more 'an two minutes to smoke that lot out."

"I can't!" said Jessica. The mere thought of involving her father in anything to do with school struck her as acutely disconcerting and bizarre. There must be something else which could be done.

"Well, if you won't go and see if he's there, I will," said Nance. "I'll nip over your fence. Which one is it, Jess?"

"The one over there by that tree."

Off bolted Nance, throwing out her long legs sideways as she ran. In a moment she had vanished round the curve of the avenue.

"If your father isn't in, she won't go and fetch the police, will she?" asked Bunny. "Mum went to bed ill last time Syd got into trouble with the police."

"Oh, don't fuss," said Jessica unsympathetically. "Nance won't call the police. She doesn't like them."

They stood there waiting; it seemed to them a very long time; but actually Nance was only gone a few minutes before she reappeared . . . with Uncle Richard.

Jessica, astonished, made a little movement towards him. But Uncle Richard's face was steely. He took no notice of her whatsoever. Indeed, she had to step sideways out of his path as he strode unseeingly past her and made straight for the house. It didn't take him a moment to spot the open conservatory door. He was through it and inside. The terrifying thing was that the uproar didn't immediately diminish with his entry; indeed, it seemed to Jessica's ears that it grew worse. He had been knocked on the head, murdered . . .

Then . . . there was utter silence.

Jessica, Nance and Bunny stood in a row marvelling at the silence. Suddenly Nance stepped up to the house, and inclined her ear.

"He's telling them off, good and proper," she said, returning to Jessica's side.

"He won't tell the police on them, will he?" asked Bunny.

"Why should he?" replied Nance. "He's used to dealing with things himself, ain't he? Look, here they come!"

But it was only Patsy Curry. She came out through the green-house door, carefully holding up her hand, which was tied up in a handkerchief already soaked with blood. When she saw Jessica, she came up to her.

"Is he your uncle? Isn't he gorgeous! Told me to hold my hand under the cold tap, he did."

The others were coming out now. One by one they emerged, silenced and ashamed. Last of all came Uncle Richard. He closed the green-house door, stared up at the house to mark the broken window, and then joined the children. The boys sheered away from him, but not so Patsy.

Jessica was glad to see that he made short work of her.

"I told you to cut off home, didn't I? Get that filthy handkerchief off and wash the cut under the cold tap. *And* keep your arm up."

Through her curtain of hair Patsy shot him one soulful glance which Uncle Richard failed to notice. Then she resigned herself, whistled to her friend Sandra, and they both ran on ahead.

The rest of them made a procession down the avenue. Uncle Richard and Nance led the way; they were discussing the laws of house-breaking. Just behind them walked Jessica and Bunny. After a wider gap came the boys, still very silent.

They were drawing near to the strawberry tree, to the bush behind which the case lay hidden. Jessica took a deep breath. She would interrupt this long conversation, ask her uncle to open the case. Whatever awful thing there was inside, he wouldn't mind; he was used to horrors in Africa. And if the awful boys crowded round and saw, he would silence them with a look. They wouldn't be able to let out those blood-curdling cries which made ghastly things more ghastly.

"Sir?"

She was too late. Charlie, after a lot of pushing and whispered encouragement, was making sure that this unusual encounter should not end here.

"You are Jess's uncle from Africa, aren't you? Will you tell us about it—about the lions and such?"

# 14

## *The Zoological Quarterly*

The next moment they were all crowding round him, asking questions, listening open-mouthed to his replies. Gradually a story-telling hush fell on them. Even Syd stood harmless for once, transported to Africa, his eyes fixed on Uncle Richard's face.

But Jessica hung back. She wanted the boys to go so that she could be alone with Uncle Richard and show him the suitcase under the tree. The idea of going to bed that night with the mystery of its contents unsolved made her shudder. She would dream of a gory head.

"Uncle ——" She pressed her way through the circle of boys and touched her uncle's sleeve.

"Hullo . . . hullo?"

"I think we ought to go home. It must be tea-time."

Uncle Richard glanced at his wrist-watch.

"Bless my soul! Half-past four. . . . Now, cut along, you lads!"

"Finish the story, sir!" they pleaded.

"Not now. Off you go, the lot of you. And don't let me find one of you in that house again. Or in the avenue.

It will take me a good day's work to patch up all the damage you've done."

"We're awfully sorry, sir."

"Thanks a lot, sir, for not splitting on us."

" 'Bye, sir."

They ran off in a bunch, bumping into each other as they turned round to wave.

"Where's your long-legged friend?" said Uncle Richard to Jessica.

But Nance had taken herself off, unnoticed. Jessica felt a stab of remorse.

"She must have gone minutes ago. Uncle . . . Uncle, could you wait a minute? There's something I want to show you."

Uncle Richard hardly paused in his long stride.

"We'll get into hot water with your mother, you know, if we stop now." Together they turned out of the avenue into the glare of the road. "What was it?"

"An old suitcase stuffed behind a bush. I did wonder . . . if there was anything in it."

"You're hopeful. I've never yet found a suitcase stuffed with bank-notes. That avenue must be quite a dumping-ground. I expect you'll find a rusty gas-stove dumped there one day, or a dressmaker's dummy."

Uncle Richard's imagination and hers did not seem to be running along the same lines at all; and even if a severed head and a dressmaker's dummy did link up in a macabre fashion, there was something rather comic in it. Suddenly Jessica felt better.

They were late for tea. Everybody, including Mr. Rendell, was seated at the tea-table.

"I'm sorry, Lydia ——" Uncle Richard came striding in, surprising everyone with his relaxed good cheer—"but Jessica and I had to eject a gang of her boy-friends from the Manor."

Jessica did not know what to make of this explanation. She sat tight, aware that everyone was looking at her.

"It's the first I've heard of Jessica's boy-friends," said Rosalind, rounding her eyes dramatically.

"Boy-friends? In the Manor? What were they doing there?" asked Mr. Rendell. "Jess, what have you been up to?"

"Richard, you had better tell us the whole story," said Mrs. Rendell quickly.

Uncle Richard, usually so shy of opening his mouth, showed no hesitation.

"I was reclining in a deck-chair in the garden after that hail-storm, when suddenly a long-legged girl came tumbling over the fence, crying, 'Help!' She said that a gang of boys had broken into the Manor and would I come and help Jessica get them out."

"But, Jessica, what had these boys to do with you?" asked Mrs. Rendell.

"They had nothing to do with me," said Jessica, hunching her shoulders to her ears.

"Darling, apparently you were there with them. Suppose you tell us exactly how you were mixed up in it."

"I was only doing what Miss Sims asked me to do."

"And what did Miss Sims ask you to do?"

"Show the strawberry tree to my form."

"Miss Sims asked *you* to show the strawberry tree to

your form! But doesn't she know that the avenue is private property? And what was she thinking of to put you in charge of a crowd of boys and girls?"

"She had been coming herself. She thought only Madeline and Rupert and me would turn up. Then she told me her mother was ill and she couldn't come."

"Well, I think she behaved very casually indeed. If she couldn't come herself, she should have sent some other adult in her place."

"Mother! Don't speak about Miss Sims like that. Her mother may be dead by now!"

There was a shocked silence at this outburst. Then Jessica's mother said gently: "Darling, I don't think that Miss Sims would have been at school on Friday if her mother were as ill as all that. Now, just tell me who these boys were who behaved so badly?"

"*Awful* boys from the fourth form. They heard about my strawberry tree from Bunny."

Mr. Rendell, who had been taking in all that Jessica had said, now pushed back his chair.

"I must be off. Cheer up, Jess. Nobody's blaming you for anything."

"Miss Sims is being blamed," said Jessica. "She should have left her dying mother."

"Don't go on about Miss Sims, darling. I am only so glad that you acted sensibly and ran to Uncle Richard for help."

"That was Nance, not me."

"A very nice girl, I thought," put in Uncle Richard.

Mrs. Rendell looked surprised.

"I'm glad you liked her. She's Jessica's friend."

"She is not my friend any longer. And you *can't* be really glad that Uncle likes her. Her father is still a dustman and beyond the pale."

There was another flabbergasted silence. Across the table Jessica met Isabel's wide stare. "She thinks I am being awful," thought Jessica. "Well, I am awful. I can't stop myself . . ."

"Jessica, darling," said her mother gravely, at last, "I know you are feeling upset when you talk in this dramatic fashion. But there is nothing to be upset about. You know I don't dislike Nance." As Jessica would not look up, Mrs. Rendell turned to her brother. "The father is a troublemaker. He's been thrown out of job after job. Nance repeats his extraordinary ideas to Jessica. That's all I have against the child."

Uncle Richard cleared his throat awkwardly.

"Look, Lydia," he said, "if you'll excuse me, I think I'll just borrow a hammer and take another look at the damage. I can't do all the repairs this evening, but I'll clear up the broken glass and see what will need doing."

The door closed on Uncle Richard whistling cheerfully.

"My!" ejaculated Rosalind. "What a transformation! He's like a dog with two tails."

"Wouldn't you be?" flared Jessica. "If you'd had absolutely nothing to do for weeks and weeks and then found something?"

"Jessica *dear*!" Mrs. Rendell placed a hand on Jessica's arm. "Now, there is something I want to ask you, if you will take it *quite* calmly. When I put a clean blouse of yours away this afternoon I came across a tin of cat's meat."

Rosalind burst out laughing. Jessica crimsoned and avoided Isabel's eyes.

"Now, Jessica, just tell me what the tin is doing hidden away in your drawer?"

"It's not doing anything. I bought it for a cat."

"Oh, Mother!" broke in Rosalind. "I guess what she's up to! She's beginning to collect food for her home for lost cats."

"Jessica, you are not!" said her mother. "I can't do with any more strays."

Isabel blushed to the roots of her hair, so violently that everybody noticed. They all stared, then glanced away, embarrassed. Mrs. Rendell said quickly:

"Isabel, I don't suppose that anyone has ever told you: but Claudius is a stray. Jessica insisted on our taking him in. She would like to tempt half the cat population of the district into this house because she thinks they're starving."

* * *

Uncle Richard was not at his usual place at the tea-table on Monday afternoon.

"He only appeared briefly at lunch-time. He's been at the Manor all day," said Mrs. Rendell.

"Good old Uncle," said Rosalind. "He is like a dog with ——"

"Don't say that again," said Jessica, putting her hands over her ears. "Mum, what do most people do when they're looking for a job?"

"Go to the Labour Exchange, or go to the Public Library and read the Vacancy columns in the papers," said Rosalind glibly.

"Your uncle does go round to the library, Jessica," said Mrs. Rendell, "but he's getting tired of never finding anything."

"Aunt Lydia," said Isabel, "would you please excuse me? I'm supposed to be round at the hair-dresser's——"

"Why, yes, Isabel, of course," said her aunt.

Isabel slipped quietly from the room. Rosalind said, when the door was shut:

"I wish she'd leave off being quite so good and polite."

"I wish she would too."

"Mummy," said Sophie, giving her mother a strange glance, "do you mean you want her to be *naughty?*"

"No, darling, but we should like her to feel a little more at home with us than she does at present."

"She writes reams and reams to that Maimie friend of hers," pointed out Rosalind.

"Mother, would you please excuse *me*?" said Jessica.

"Why, are you in a hurry to get to your homework?"

"I want to go out."

"Out? Where?"

"I know where she wants to go," said Rosalind triumphantly. "She wants to go round to the library to look through the Vacancy columns."

Mrs. Rendell turned a brooding gaze on Jessica. Jessica leaned back in her chair and looked as if she would burst before admitting that such was the case.

"Darling, you will only be wasting your time . . ."

"*And* getting in the way of other people," said Rosalind.

"Mother . . ."

"Very well, darling," said Mrs. Rendell.

Jessica shot out of the house like a bolt.

The public reading-room of the library looked like an enormous class-room. There were rows and rows of desk-like tables on which lay magazines, but the people who sat at them were most of them elderly and one or two were asleep. The newspapers were displayed on stands ranged round the walls. People stood to read them. Jessica hesitated, confused by the hush and the stuffiness and the unfamiliar surroundings. Each of the newspapers seemed to have a reader standing in front of it, and she remembered Rosalind's words, "You will only be in the way." Then she saw a man moving off from one of them. As she made her way quickly towards the free place she passed by an old tramp who was sprawling at one of the magazine tables, his head sunk in his arms. Suddenly he raised his head, muttered something unintelligible at Jessica, and glared at her with a pair of wild blue eyes.

"What?" said Jessica.

But the tramp, startled out of his dream, saw nothing familiar in Jessica's face, and he mumbled shamefacedly and buried his head in his arms again.

Thoroughly shaken, Jessica made the rest of her way to the newspaper. But by now someone else had slipped in front of it and was turning the pages. Apparently the only thing to do was to queue. She stood patiently by the elbow of a man studying *The Guardian*. Once or twice he cast her a glance of annoyance, and Jessica was rapidly losing her courage, when he turned on his heel and walked off.

Now . . .

There were columns and columns of vacancies. Amongst all that lot there must be something. . . . She would be thorough, let nothing escape her. She would run her finger down the columns from A to Z. . . .

Assistant Matron . . . assistant Nannie . . . assistant . . .

Somebody coughed at Jessica's elbow.

Book-keeper, male or female . . .

"When you've quite finished, miss. . . ." said a man's voice in her ear.

Jessica gave the speaker a scared glance, and moved away, defeated.

Where else could she look? A smallish newspaper, with nobody standing in front of it, proved to be *The Poulterers' Times*. Jessica turned her back on it to give a last desperate glance round the room. Immediately her eye was arrested by a seated figure, so different from anyone else in the reading-room, but so familiar with its sleek fair hair hanging forward, that for a second she just stood and gaped. Then she ran up to her.

"Isabel!"

Isabel started violently. She quickly closed the magazine she was studying, and put her arm across the cover.

"Jessica!"

"What are you doing here?"

Jessica took a hasty look at the magazine as she spoke, but the black cloth binder told her nothing.

"What are *you* doing?" countered Isabel.

"Trying to find a job for Uncle Richard."

". . . So am I."

Jessica took another glance at the black cover.

"*I* was looking through the newspapers."

"Well, I was looking through the advertisements in the—*The Zoological Quarterly*."

How clever of Isabel to know where to look.

"Have you found anything?"

"No. Have you?"

"No. Let's give it up."

Isabel rose without a word and they went out of the building together. They walked along the street side by side, but leaving a gap between them. Jessica felt that Isabel had been startled and put out by her sudden appearance. They spoke stiffly and politely across the gap.

"Fancy us both having the same idea," said Jessica. "Kind of telepathy."

"Yes, kind of, I suppose."

"I feel awful about Uncle Richard."

"So do I."

"Just hanging around with nothing to do all day, and knowing that Mother can't think up another single job for him. He doesn't ask as much as he used to. I suppose he feels a menace."

"I think it's absolutely beastly for him!"

Jessica bridged the gap with a startled glance.

"You mean . . . rather beastly for him being with *us*?"

"Oh no, of course not. He's terribly lucky to have such nice relations!"

But Jessica did not know how to take this outburst either. Was this a subtle hint that Uncle Richard as a genuine relative of the family was in a far more enviable position than one who was merely an adopted relative? Aware of dangerous currents, Jessica splashed wildly round for safer waters.

"Those poor old men asleep in the library."

"What about them?"

The tone was brittle; but Jessica went bravely on.

"Don't laugh, but I'm now wondering if I shouldn't give up the idea of a home for stray cats and run a home for tramps instead."

"But, Jessica——" across the gap Isabel's eyes looked into hers, unhappy, challenging—"why don't you want to paint? You're so good at painting."

"Oh, I do want to paint. But I feel so sorry for cats and tramps."

"I really don't think you need be. Tramps don't like having a house to live in—that's why they tramp. It's just silly and—and sentimental giving people what they don't want, and giving animals things which you think they ought to like, but don't."

Isabel hadn't raised her voice at all, but it was extraordinary how great was the silence in the street when she stopped talking. Jessica had to actually look at the traffic in order to make sure that it was still roaring by.

"I see . . ." said Jessica at last.

"There's nothing to see," said Isabel. "It's just what I think about tramps. Don't go and . . ." She broke off and didn't seem to know how to go on. Then suddenly she said, "Wait . . ." and she stopped in front of a sweet-shop window. There was a very long pause while Isabel regarded the sweets in the bottles and the little heaps of chocolates and bon-bons on silver trays.

"If *you* had to choose, which would you go for?" she finally asked.

"Oh, gosh . . ." said Jessica. "I like anything. I like those sweets there."

Isabel led the way into the shop. One foot over the

threshold she paused and said in a voice, both casual and confiding—just as if there had never been any gap between them—"Oh, by the way, don't say anything to Uncle Richard about my looking in the *Zoological Quarterly*. Don't—don't please say *anything* to him about it, Jess."

# 15

## *Please Yourself*

On Wednesday morning, just three days before the garden party at "The Limes", Sophie sneezed at breakfast over her cornflakes. Nobody took any notice, except her mother, who said, "Bless you". A moment later, Sophie gave two more sneezes which she did her best to smother. Then five minutes later she gave three very violent ones.

Sophie stared frightened at her mother, unable to look away.

"Darling, you're not starting a cold!"

Sophie shook her head vehemently.

"No sore throat?"

Sophie shook her head again.

Mr. and Mrs. Rendell now exchanged glances.

"It may be only a touch of hay-fever," said Mr. Rendell. "I'll run her down to school this morning and we'll call at the chemist and get some tablets." He stood up and held out his hand. "Come along, Sophie."

"I haven't got a cold—or anything," said Sophie stubbornly.

"No, darling. But just do as Daddy says."

Sophie hesitated a second; then followed her father with quiet dignity. Rosalind said: "Poor Sophie! The world will come to an end if she can't do 'The Pied Piper' on Saturday."

Jessica licked the honey spoon and then dreamily regarded the result, and spoke.

"Sophie is the most precious thing in the house. She is above rubies."

Mrs. Rendell took the spoon briskly from Jessica. Uncle Richard said: "I seem to have been done out of a job this morning. Jessica, I'll walk along with you."

Jessica was delighted. Uncle Richard helped to clear the breakfast table. He carried a pyramid of three cups and saucers carefully into the kitchen.

"Have you finished patching up the damage at the Manor?" asked Jessica, as they turned out of the gate together.

"Yes, worse luck. I suppose I mustn't hope any more boys break into it. As it is I feel I'm not really within the law in covering up for your boy-friends. We must keep it strictly under our hats."

Uncle Richard had certainly relaxed a lot since the incident at the Manor. This was the longest sentence he had ever said to her. It was a shame that the future stretched before him like an arid desert.

"How's your friend Nance?" he asked suddenly.

"I think she's all right."

"Haven't made it up yet?"

Jessica said nothing.

"I never saw anybody fall over a fence so quickly. She seemed to operate in a whirl of arms and legs."

This was such a good description of Nance that Jessica left off feeling awkward and burst out laughing.

"Hulloa!" exclaimed Uncle Richard. "Isn't that her just turning out of Brightwell Road?"

True enough it was Nance. She had appeared round the corner of her road, and in a moment she would reach the further side of the crossing which Jessica and her uncle were approaching.

Uncle Richard quickened his pace. "Come on. Over we go." He grasped Jessica's hand. His keen eye and long legs had Jessica through a gap in the traffic before she knew where she was. "Good morning," he said, and raised his hat to Nance.

Nance blushed, beamed and opened her mouth. Whether she really had anything to say for herself was never to be known, for Uncle Richard gave her no time. He said briskly, "Well, I'll leave you two to go on together," grinned quite wickedly at Jessica, raised his hat again to Nance and strode off.

Nance stood there, gazing after him.

"Isn't he lovely!" she exclaimed.

Her whole-hearted admiration made Jessica forget all the awkwardness between them.

"Oh, Nance, if only I could find him a job!"

Nance walked along with her just as she used to.

"Didn't know he was looking for one. Thought he was home on leave or something like that."

"He's left Africa, but nobody wants him here as he only knows about wild animals. He's tried the Zoo."

Nance formed her lips into a judicious whistle.

"What about a circus?"

"Oh no! That wouldn't do at all!"

"Too posh, I suppose."

"Don't say that!" But it wasn't the moment to show annoyance now that they were back on friendly terms again. "I mean, I just don't think he'd like dressing up in tights and making a tiger jump through a hoop."

"H'mm. Perhaps not . . . I know, Jess!"

"What?"

"The very thing! Why shouldn't he go round giving lectures to schools about his wild animals? Those boys didn't half like him the other day. And he hadn't half got some good yarns."

"But how do you get that sort of job?"

"I don't rightly know—but he could come to our school for a start, couldn't he? Look, Jess, you tell Mr. Berryman about him."

"Me? . . . tell Mr. Berryman?"

"Why not? He's matey and he does listen. He even listens to me sometimes."

"But—but wouldn't it be rather a—a queer thing to say to him?"

"How do you mean—queer?"

"Asking him to give my uncle a job. He'd be so—so taken aback."

"Goodness, I wouldn't let a thing like that worry me. If your uncle was my uncle, and I wanted to find him a job, I'd try anything."

As Jessica remained silent, Nance took a quick look at her face.

"But you please yerself. I'm not egging you on to do

nothing—not after that fuss I got you into over that Freedom from Hunger game."

Nance sounded distinctly huffy. Jessica hesitated, and then said timidly:

"You're sure it's a good idea?"

"I think it's a good idea all right. But if you don't, that's the end of it."

Jessica was filled with dismay. Even if Nance's idea was a good one, she, Jessica, felt thoroughly unnerved at the thought of putting it into practice. She stole a glance at Nance's chilly profile. She had never known her like this before.

"I—I say, Nance, I never thanked you for—for coming to my rescue last Saturday."

Nance faced round on her, stony.

"Why should you thank me?"

"Well, Mother ——"

"Ah, it was her!"

"Yes."

"It ain't nothing to do with her. If I choose to keep that Syd off of you, it's because . . . because . . ."

"Because what?"

But Nance's face went hard again. She stomped on ahead a little; and then thought better of it. She swung round on Jessica, and exclaimed, "For pete's sake, cheer up. I thought you wanted me to suggest something for your uncle, and so I did. But you don't like the idea, so forget about it."

But Jessica couldn't forget about it. The suggestion had been made, and there it was, wriggling deeper and deeper into her mind. She sat in her desk nervously considering Mr. Berryman. He had flung himself into the class-room with his usual clumsy zest. He was off now about the school sports, and when that was finished with he would be on to collecting the dinner money, and when that had been mastered—Mr. Berryman was hopeless with money and somebody always had to add up for him—he would switch on to something else. Even when he paused for breath, you could see his beady eyes darting towards the next thing. Hold him up with some story of an uncle . . . wild animals . . . a lecture, and he would stare, hesitate, try hard not to look at a complete loss. Worse, he might even look embarrassed. After all, it would be embarrassing having to listen to one of his class cadging a job for an out-of-work uncle.

The very idea made Jessica press her knuckles into her hot cheeks.

But, on the other hand, if she said nothing, could she ever look Nance in the face again? Or her uncle for that matter? She would have two guilty secrets instead of one: not only the out-of-date postal order, but the knowledge that she had, out of sheer funk and embarrassment, made no attempt whatsoever to put Nance's suggestion to Mr. Berryman.

The bell for assembly pealed along the corridors. In the middle of a sentence Mr. Berryman broke off, cried, "Oh, hell's bells!" and banged shut his register. Everybody stood up, left their desks and formed a line to the door. Now was the moment; now or never.

Jessica slipped out of her place in the line and stood by Mr. Berryman's desk, mouth open, ready, so that when he looked up . . .

Mr. Berryman looked up.

"Oh . . . yes, you'll do, Jessica. Shoot down for me with this list to Mr. Crosbie. If he's gone, leave it on his bench in the lab."

A paper was stuffed into Jessica's hand. Before she knew what she was doing, she was out in the corridor. Her chance had gone. . . .

Her chance for the whole day had gone. Mr. Berryman took no lessons with his own class on Thursdays. Unless he was on playground duty or dinner duty she might not see him again until tomorrow.

Mr. Berryman appeared neither on playground duty nor on dinner duty. At first Jessica did not know whether to feel relieved or sorry. After all, if he wasn't there, she couldn't ask him, could she? It was out of her hands. But Nance was eyeing her from the other end of the dinner table. She did not grin or wink as she usually did, just gave her a single look of enquiry and then, because Jessica signalled nothing back in return, looked away.

Well, what did Nance expect her to do, for goodness sake? Hadn't she seen her trying to speak to Mr. Berryman this morning and being pushed off before she could get a word out? Did she expect her now to beard him in some distant class-room with forty strange boys and girls listening all ears to what she stammered out, or to hang about the staff-room, holy of holies, trying to waylay him on his way in or out? Have a heart. . . .

Yes: that was exactly what she would expect. Nance was on the side of Uncle Richard, dazzled by the way he had raised his hat so nicely to her and smiled. Girls were all alike.

Jessica slouched hang-dog into the studio for Art lesson. She stuck up her easel as far away from Nance as possible. She did not feel as she usually felt when she unscrewed the tops of her little row of poster paints. And she would not look up and stand aside when Miss Giles came round to inspect her painting. She just went on pretending she wasn't there.

Miss Giles looked, and went on her way without speaking.

"I am an outcast," thought Jessica, savage and miserable.

"Jessica," said Miss Giles at the end of the afternoon, "be a kind girl and wash those dirty palettes for me."

It was not surprising that Miss Giles had asked Jessica, for although Jessica was very unwilling to do any washing-up at home she was always delighted to oblige at school, especially if it was for Miss Giles. But this afternoon she held the palettes under the studio tap without a word and dried them on a towel without a word and stacked them up on the window-sill still without a word. Miss Giles glanced at her now and again, but said nothing. She was not the sort of person to ask what the matter was, but when Jessica had finished and picked up her satchel in the now empty studio, she said, "Thank you, Jessica," in a very kind voice.

Well, one good thing about that, Nance would have gone home by now and she would be spared any more of her solemn, enquiring glances. But if Syd was hanging about . . . Jessica's heart thumped. Would it be wise to hurry . . . or not to hurry? She decided to walk slowly along the corridor.

But who was that crossing the vestibule ahead of her, hands thrust into pockets, teeth clenched round a pipe?

"Mr. Berryman! Mr. Berryman!"

Jessica dashed along the corridor, reached the vestibule and skipped sideways across his path to intercept him.

"Mr. Berryman . . ."

"Hullo!" Mr. Berryman stopped and took his pipe out of his mouth.

"I tried to speak to you this morning, but you wouldn't give me a chance!"

"I'm sorry about that. What can I do for you now?"

It was far easier to indignantly accuse Mr. Berryman of not listening to her than to say what she had to say.

"Mr. Berryman, I've got an uncle . . ."

"Yes?" Mr. Berryman couldn't have looked more ready and enquiring. She had to go on somehow.

"He's a Game Warden—at least, he was. Now he's staying with us and—and Nance thought . . . Well, you know *you* said how dull the lectures had been this year, and he's—he's awfully good at talking about wild animals."

"Ah . . ." Mr. Berryman looked as if he had cottoned on to the idea at once. "He lectures on animals, does he?"

"Well, no, not *yet* . . ."

"But he's willing to have a shot?"

This sounded more than hopeful.

"I'm sure he is," said Jessica, with fervour.

"But you haven't actually asked him?"

"Oh no. I couldn't say anything to him first. If—if you didn't want him, it would only be another disappointment."

What exactly Mr. Berryman made of this it would be difficult to say. He hesitated just a fraction of a moment, and then said, in very brisk, very cheerful and very pleasant tones:

"Well now, the person you really want to tackle over this is the Head. You see, arranging about lectures and things isn't really my pigeon. You want the fountain-head."

"Me? Go to Mr. Stephens?"

"Why not? He's always asking you boys and girls to go to him with your ideas. You go to him straight now and say to him exactly what you've said to me."

Jessica took a step backwards.

"He'll have gone home by now."

"Oh no, he won't. School doesn't end for him at four o'clock. Run along quick and you'll catch him all right."

Mr. Berryman put his hand on Jessica's shoulder and turned her round to face the curving staircase which led to the Head's room. He gave her a little push. And then not only that, he stood there watching her, so that when Jessica, moving doubtfully off and with a foot on the first step, turned round, he was still watching her, the pipe back in his mouth again, grinning.

Jessica walked up the staircase very slowly to show her utter reluctance. It was the main staircase and one which she hardly ever used as it did not lead to any of the class-rooms she frequented. Its wide steps and the curve of its hand-rail were like those of a palace staircase, and added to the solemnity of the occasion. And the corridor at the top was deserted and impressively silent. The door, just at the end on the right, showed its system of coloured lights. The red and yellow signs were dull, lifeless, the green . . . the green was lit up. Jessica stood in front of the door. What was she going to say? "Say just what you said to me," Mr. Berryman had exhorted her. Could he see her now, hesitating, frightened? With an awful feeling of being compelled to do something which she lacked the courage to do, Jessica lifted her hand to knock.

At that precise instant the green round darkened, the yellow flashed out.

What did that mean, that he was going home? That in a minute or two he would open the door and brush past her: unless she intercepted him? Jessica took a step to the side and waited. Her heart thumped. She waited one minute . . . two minutes. Then the yellow light went out.

They were all out now, all three. He had gone: he had gone by some other door.

# 16

## *Isabel's Strange Behaviour*

By the time Jessica arrived in the cloakroom, the pegs allotted to 11A were all empty. In fact the cloakroom itself was empty except for a group of senior girls just clattering out on their high heels. Jessica snatched up her beret in a panic. She did not like the silence, the spectral iron pegs. She did not like being the very last. It added to her sense of failure. Because she had failed.

One good thing was that Nance hadn't waited for her. The milling crowds who hung about the school gates had gone home. Only the five girls remained, each with a foot on the pedal of her bicycle, calling last words to the others before riding purposefully away.

How nice to breeze confidently down the hill without a care in the world. Jessica mooched along, dangling her satchel by its strap, letting it go bump, bump against her legs. . . .

Sophie had stopped sneezing. Jessica found her in bed, propped up with three pillows, her dark hair brushed neatly across her brow. She stared at Jessica over the top of *The Borrowers*.

"I'm not ill. I'm resting."

Jessica felt that Sophie existed like some prima donna, so gifted and so fragile that she lived a life of special arrangements. She stumped downstairs and found nobody at the tea-table. She sat down and took a slice of cake. Her mother came in with the tea-pot.

"Why, Jess, you are late back. Everybody is late today: Rosalind and Isabel have a Geographical Society meeting."

"Where's Uncle?"

"He's fixing up a shelf in the garage."

What a mercy. It would have been the last straw to find him staring hopelessly out of the window.

A door banged, and Rosalind burst in on them. She kissed her mother boisterously, and cried, "Isabel is already a celebrity!"

"What are you talking about?" said her mother. "Tell me."

"Isabel has been asked to read a paper on the Fawcett expedition to Brazil to the Geographical Society. Nobody else in the Lower Fifth has ever been given such an honour. Miss Kelly thinks she's the cat's whiskers."

"Why, Isabel, I am pleased," said Mrs. Rendell warmly.

For once Isabel's pretty manners deserted her. She muttered and looked down. Rosalind glanced at her, a bit dashed, and then said, in rather flattened tones:

"I wish Isabel could be pleased."

"Aunt Lydia," said Isabel quickly, "I haven't time. I told them I hadn't time. Nobody listened."

"We all thought she was being bashful," said Rosalind,

"because of the honour. It would have taken *my* breath away."

"I expect Isabel was taken completely by surprise. But she'll feel better about it when she's had some tea and is feeling less tired. It's all this heat." Mrs. Rendell glanced very kindly at her niece. "Won't you, Isabel?"

"No, Aunt Lydia, honestly, I don't want to do it. It would take me ages and ages, and I'm all behind with my work as it is."

Jessica gaped and listened. She had never seen Isabel look so worked up before.

"Isabel dear, it can't be as bad as all that," her mother was saying, "or you wouldn't be getting such good marks."

"She's just over-fussy and conscientious," cried Rosalind, putting her arm round Isabel's waist.

"I'm not!"

"Mother, I think Isa works too hard and worries too much. Yes, I do. And there's no reason why she should get so worked up about it. We help each other with our languages and maths and get on like a house on fire. We're a team."

"It's the Biology, Aunt Lydia. Now that we're on to ——"

"Oh, Mum, that's just the one subject I can't help her with. Oh, I do wish I'd decided to take Biology for my O-level. Daddy wanted me to take it. I suppose Miss Lyall wouldn't let me swop over to it after all. I bet I could soon mug it up and ——"

"Be quiet just a minute, Rosalind. Isabel dear, there's no need for you to take Biology, if you're beginning to find it so difficult. You've got enough subjects for your O-level ——"

"But I don't want to give it up," said Isabel, looking frightened and stubborn.

"But Isa, you old goose, you've just said you don't like it!" cried Rosalind.

"I never said I didn't like it. I said I found it difficult."

"Well, I still think you an awful old goose to go on doing it when you needn't. Geography is your star turn. I don't see why you need worry about passing your O-level anyhow. You're so bright at essays, all you need do is to write your travels and you'd be a best-seller. . . ."

A voice issued from Jessica's mouth. She was as much surprised as anybody else to hear it.

"Shut up, shut up. Why can't you just let her do what she wants to do?"

There was a dead silence from everybody.

"Jess!" exclaimed her mother.

"Well, why don't you?" muttered Jessica. She looked at Isabel for confirmation, half-expecting a glance of relief, but Isabel's eyes showed nothing but alarm. "Why can't you keep quiet!" they seemed to say.

Mrs. Rendell put her hand on Isabel's shoulder.

"Be a kind girl and see if Sophie wants anything more to eat," she said.

"Mother," burst out Rosalind as soon as Isabel had run off, "I was so pleased for Isabel!"

"Well, darling, if *she*'s not pleased. . . . And you shouldn't really have said that about her travels. She's so terribly sensitive about not being in her own home."

Rosalind rounded her eyes and pressed her hands over her mouth.

"She doesn't like *any* of us," said Jessica.

Uncle Richard came in whistling, unaware of hurt feelings, unaware that Isabel had been tactfully sent off on an errand, oblivious of tension in the atmosphere.

"I've fixed that job, Lydia. Actually I've put up a couple. They'll do for some of those seed-boxes out of the potting-shed."

Jessica held her breath. Everyone knew Daddy didn't like the garage being turned into an overflow for the potting-shed. Luckily all her mother said was: "Oh, thank you, Rick."

Isabel slipped quietly back into the room. She had combed her hair and changed her frock. Without glancing at anyone she got out her homework.

"I'm sorry I've been so long, Aunt Lydia. I've put Sophie's tray in the kitchen. She doesn't want anything more to eat."

"That's fine, dear. Thank you."

Uncle Richard stood in front of the window. He still whistled under his breath, but depression was catching up on him, washing over him again.

Jessica slunk off, conscience-stricken. If only she'd had the courage to speak to Mr. Stephens. . . . Would Mr. Berryman ask her on Monday what luck she had had? In a way she had failed not only her uncle, but Mr. Berryman too. He had waved her on so nicely with his pipe.

She dragged off her school frock and changed into her jeans. Astride the fence at the bottom of the garden, she let the hush of the avenue steal over her. How still the trees were! The midges were crazy to dance round and round like that when not even a bird disturbed that dark, green silence.

But the suitcase. She had forgotten all about it. Was that lying where she had last seen it, hidden between the thicket and the fence? What a good moment this might have been to solve the mystery of its grisly contents! Had she been feeling absolutely at ease with her uncle, she could have run back into the house, seized him by the hand and let him destroy the horror of *not* knowing. Besides, it would have given him something to do, filled up ten minutes of his empty time.

Empty time.... And still nothing stirred in the avenue. Sunken, silent, with all its trees heavy with the dark leaves of summer, it kept its secret to itself.

# 17

# *The Garden Party*

Saturday morning came: the day of the Garden Party. Jessica planted her bare elbows on the breakfast table and languidly ate toast, enjoying the cool morning air on her arms and legs. It was a pity, she thought, that the morning freshness couldn't be extended throughout the day. She could sit here indefinitely.

But this was Sophie's great day. Pale, dark-eyed and brittle, she was being coaxed by her mother to drink another half-cup of coffee.

"I hope there will be plenty of strawberry ices," said Rosalind. "Oh, Isa, I am glad you can come with us. You will be tickled to death with the Miss Fanshawes. And I shall revel in nostalgia, pointing out to you the scenes of my kindergarten days."

"It's very kind of the Miss Fanshawes to let us all come. We'll be quite a large party. Jessica dear, don't forget that you will be expected to help with the refreshments with all the other 'old girls'. Don't let me find you occupying one of the few deck-chairs."

"I'll wear my jeans and then it won't matter if I spill anything."

"You will wash yourself thoroughly before you go," said her mother, "and wear your blue linen frock."

Jessica groaned and then glanced at Isabel to see if she was registering sympathy or appraisal. But Isabel wasn't looking at anybody; and she was only playing with her breakfast.

At lunch Isabel left a lot of her salad and refused the pudding altogether.

"Why, Isabel dear, haven't you any appetite?" asked her aunt.

"I've got a headache, Aunt Lydia."

"A headache shouldn't take away your appetite," said Rosalind. "It is your head that aches, not your tummy."

Mr. Rendell glanced at his niece.

"This heat's too much for most people. And I think you've been working too hard, young lady. Suppose you lie down for an hour with an aspirin. Then if you feel like getting up in time for the Garden Party . . ."

"Oh, but she must!" cried Rosalind.

"There's no must about it. The streets will be broiling hot by the afternoon, and if Isabel doesn't feel up to it, she'll do no good traipsing out in the sun."

"I will stay at home with her and bring her up a cup of tea at four o'clock," announced Jessica firmly. The idea of doing something quite different from the rest of the family had a quite uncanny appeal.

"Oh no . . . honestly! I expect I shall sleep and sleep, and not want *anything*. I'd hate anybody to stay in because of me. I'd *rather* be alone!"

Isabel sounded quite distressed. She disregarded Jessica and spoke only to her aunt.

"All right, Isa dear, if you don't mind being on your own . . ."

"I *don't*, not a bit. I don't *want* Jessica to miss the Garden Party . . ."

Jessica pulled a small face. She wished she'd kept her mouth shut. Isabel seemed to hate her guts.

When Jessica went upstairs to change for the Garden Party Isabel was still lying on her bed in a darkened room which smelt of eau-de-cologne. She heard Rosalind breeze in on her, drag open a curtain and chatter away in her clear and cheery voice. Through the open doors she could not quite make out Isabel's replies, but everything that Rosalind said was clear enough.

"Poor old Isa. . . . It does seem a pity to miss all the fun just for a headache. Oh, well. . . . Isa, if you're truly not coming, so won't be wanting it yourself, would you be an angel and lend me your crystal necklace?"

What an old cadger Rosalind was. . . .

"It's *not* in your cedar-wood box? . . . Then, where is it? Can't I find it? . . . Oh well, it doesn't matter. . . ."

Jessica combed her fringe, tongue between her teeth. Dolling oneself up for a frizzing garden party struck her as the last word in misdirected energy.

"There's to be raspberries with ice-cream," said Sophie behind her.

Sophie was ready, even to her silver bracelet. She sat herself on the end of her bed, waiting. Zero hour made her feel funny and remote; but she wished that her sister had greater respect for the occasion.

"Free?" Jessica demanded.

"The teas are free, but the raspberries you have to pay for. It's one-and-six."

"*Gosh*! I wish you'd told me before. I spent too much this morning. I am unfortunate." Jessica snatched up her pouch-purse and counted through its contents. "This is all bespoke for church and charities and comics. Mum will be wild if I use it. I've only got a shilling I can take from here. Then there's that threepence in my blazer pocket somewhere . . ."

Sophie opened her own little leather handbag and extracted a threepenny bit from its inner purse. Suddenly she looked like the dear little angel that most people thought her to be. Jessica's heart warmed towards her.

"Oh, Sophie, you really *are* an angel! I'll give it you back next Saturday, cross my heart."

"Children! It's time we started," called Mrs. Rendell from the foot of the stairs.

Rosalind called a bright goodbye to Isabel and came out banging the door behind her. She cast a motherly glance at Sophie who had emerged from her room, her eyes big, her jaw set, and ushered her down the stairs in front of her. Jessica brought up the rear. Her blazer *should* be hanging in the lobby. . . . There *should* be threepence in the pocket. . . .

She darted into the lobby, ignoring the waiting party in the hall. Four of the pegs were overloaded with burberries and plastic macintoshes; the fifth had nothing on it but Jessica's dark red blazer.

Now that was funny. She remembered sticking it only yesterday over Isabel's pure white rain-coat and wondering as she did so whether Isabel would mind her rather shabby blazer draped on top of it. Oh dear, she had minded. . . .

"Jessica! . . . What is that child doing?"

Jessica emerged weighty with her thoughts. The party set out: her mother and Uncle Richard in front, Rosalind and Sophie hand-in-hand behind them, Jessica lagging in the rear.

Mum had had her hair done for the occasion in a kind of Grecian twist; her shallow, wide-brimmed hat revealed the scooped-up knot; she had a smashing parasol and handbag to match. Uncle Richard wore his hat as he always did, set at an angle between the straight and the rakish. Jessica gazed at them with awe while her mind made little runs and leaps in various directions.

"Is there something funny going on . . . or isn't there? She did sound so upset and . . . urgent about me *not* staying at home. Is she . . .? Is she . . .? The rain-coat has gone, the necklace . . . the hidden SUITCASE was ready. . . . But where would she be going? Had she found herself a job somewhere? Was *that* what she was looking for that evening in the library. . . . Why hide the magazine if she was really looking on Uncle Richard's behalf?"

Jessica scuffled a pebble with her foot, head bent. Should she give voice to her suspicions? She imagined the hold-up it would cause. Sharp questions, her own halting answers: all of them standing there wondering whether to believe her queer story . . . while Sophie, speechless, grew paler and paler. Finally Mum would decide to rush back . . . only to find Isabel innocently asleep in her bed. Upset, relieved, and very cross with *her*, Jessica, she would set off again to "The Limes" only to arrive too late for "The Pied Piper". . . .

On the other hand, just suppose that Mother did find Isabel hurrying downstairs, in the very act of running away? If Isabel was unhappy, hated them all, hated living with them, why should she, Jessica, who *understood*, split on her?

"Jessica, leave that pebble alone. When will you be your age, child?"

"The Limes" appeared in view. Each time that Jessica saw it, the house behind its row of lime trees seemed still more like a picture in a Victorian story book. This was because of the new buildings springing up around it, and throwing into ever-increasing contrast the old grey stucco, the low roof, the conservatory, the lawns, the rose pergola, the shrubbery. The lawn on one side of the house was called the school lawn, and here Jessica had learnt "Farmer Brown's Dog" and "Gathering Peascods" and helped to scuff the ground bare beneath the swing. The other lawn usually held a tennis court and was bordered on two sides by a tunnel of rambler roses and on the third by netted raspberry canes. It was on this second lawn that chairs had been set out for the entertainment. Sophie had already disappeared, whisked behind the line of hessian curtains and screens which shut off from view the approach from the house to the "stage". Already the scene was lively with parents and children. Rosalind suddenly waved excitedly and ran up to a group of Grammar School girls, ex-pupils like herself. Jessica stood stolid, a disgrace; nobody from "The Limes" ever went to the Secondary Modern. If they didn't go to the

Grammar they went to the sort of boarding school where you kept your own pony. . . .

"And how's Jessica?"

Miss Sybil Fanshawe, tall, vivacious, a little cadaverous, had paused expressly to speak to her.

"I'm fine, thanks. And you, how are you keeping?" Jessica knew all the social phrases, from hearing them in constant use by her mother and Rosalind.

"Getting old, Jessica." Miss Sybil made it sound a bond between them. "And how's the painting?"

"Oh, I splash about."

Miss Sybil widened her fine, dramatic old eyes.

"Splash about?"

"Well, we have to use lots and lots of paint and enormous brushes. But I do come out top."

"Splendid, Jessica."

Miss Sybil knew, alas, that Jessica was no scholastic laurel for the school, but she spoke with warmth. She had always had a soft spot for idle, scowling Jessica, who could suddenly look up at her with such an open, understanding expression on her face.

Off she went, clapping her hands sharply, drawing about her rather long skirt a cluster of five-year-olds who gazed up at her, mouths open. Then she shooed them away to sit cross-legged in front of the first row of chairs, while Jessica watched, lost in a dream of childhood. Had she *ever* been as young as that?

The chairs were filling up. Mother and Uncle Richard, thank goodness, looked as nice as anybody. The hessian screens bulged dangerously as activities accelerated behind them. Jessica could see the head and neck of Miss

Laura Fanshawe well above it. A small figure in stiff white gauze and holding a wreath of tiny flowers could be seen darting past a big gap in the hessian. Vanessa. How silly she was going to look if she danced her classical solo clutching a wreath.

Jessica suddenly stopped staring and looked more briskly about her. She must put herself *somewhere*—but where? She was the odd man out. Nobody seemed to take any notice of her, not even her friends of a year ago, sitting heads together in a cluster on the grass, a little apart from the chairs.

And what was Isabel doing now? At this very, very moment where was she?

All eyes were on the stage. Chewing a blade of grass, Jessica slipped into the chequered gloom of the rose tunnel. Great clusters of Dorothy Perkins hid her from view, she hoped. She walked nonchalantly, just in case anyone saw the glint of her frock. A sudden burst of clapping made her feel safe; each doting parent would be agog to spot its own offspring. A narrow path forking right led her between the netted raspberries and the kitchen garden, very quiet and smelling of herbs and the compost heap. A door in the very old brick wall opened when she tried its handle, and led her out into the road.

She had no idea what she meant to do. She didn't think; she just ran. The Saturday streets were hot and stale with the fag-end of exhausted shoppers, a different world from "The Limes". She crossed the High Street, fled down the length of Russell's Road, turned into the quiet of Thorpe Avenue. It was short, and she walked along it to regain her breath. Then there was only Park Avenue and the Crescent . . . and home.

Isabel was coming up the road towards her.

Jessica's heart gave a jump. She stopped dead. So it *was* true.

Isabel had also stopped. She even put down the case she was carrying as if all her strength had been knocked out of her. Then she picked it up again, and hurried forward, crying, "You haven't told them? They don't know?"

"Oh, Isabel, where are you going?"

"Don't try and stop me!"

Jessica knew determination when she saw it.

"How can I stop you?"

"Oh, Jessica!" Isabel weakened suddenly and looked as if she were about to burst into tears. But she tightened her grip on her case, and began to walk a little faster.

"I'll help you carry your case," said Jessica.

"No, I'll carry it. The train is at three-thirty and the train up to Edinburgh at five. I'll just do it . . . before *they* find out."

"Oh, Isabel . . ."

What else could she say? They walked in silence until they reached the road leading to the station, then Jessica managed to take the case from Isabel's fingers. Yes, it was *the* case.

"I saw it behind the tree . . ."

"That's how you guessed?"

"Oh no, I thought there was a bodiless head in it. Other things made me guess."

"It was Maimie's idea before I left Edinburgh. She

liked thinking up schemes. She said, leave a case in readiness somewhere hidden, and the money for your fare, and then if things get too awful . . ."

"Oh, Isabel, *was* it so awful?"

"I didn't mean that. I'm sorry. I don't know what I mean."

The wide approach to the station was full of taxis. The air already smelt of trains. A big clock on the tower held Isabel's desperate and determined stare.

"We've got ten minutes."

Jessica bought a platform ticket and hurried after Isabel, who had already passed through the barrier. They toiled up and down steps to the London platform. Isabel sank quickly on to a seat as if her legs had given way beneath her.

"Jessica, I've left a note for Aunt Lydia."

"Yes, Isa."

"I've tried to explain, but there was so much I couldn't. I *couldn't* say how I hated never being alone . . . because of Uncle Richard. And then one 'stray cat' was all right, but the two of us were too much for anyone. And then Rosalind—oh, I know she's been terribly nice to me. And then wanting to be a nurse. It was that most of all. I felt myself getting trapped. Oh, I do like knowing all about foreign countries, but I don't want to go on to the University and do Geography. I *must* be a nurse. But it's not just that. It's everything."

Isabel broke off. With horror Jessica watched her eyes fill with tears.

"You'll be all right in Edinburgh. It'll be easier. I'm sure Mum will understand."

"I'm not even sure about Edinburgh. I don't want to be anywhere, except back where I was. And that's all over."

"I see. I knew you hated being with us."

Isabel swallowed. "It isn't anything to do with *you*. Honestly."

"I thought you—hated me."

"Oh Jessica! It was just . . . that I thought you'd guess, and I had to shut you up quick. . . . That time at the library—there's no such thing as 'The Zoological Quarterly'. I was looking in 'The Nursing Mirror'. I thought ——" She broke off, and said in a quick, frightened voice, "Is that the train?"

They stood up, and moved nearer the edge of the platform. There was the train in the distance. Both watched it getting bigger. Suddenly Isabel seized one of Jessica's fingers and held it tight: held it against the horror of stations and farewells and going off alone. A signal fell with a clack. For a second it seemed as if the train was going to roar its way through the station without stopping. Then the passing carriages slowed up; stopped. Isabel's grip tightened.

"Jess, I always liked you best. *Much* the best."

Jessica, overwhelmed, wrestled with a carriage door. In her darkest moments she would remember this. "There's room in here," she said.

Isabel pushed her case inside and then climbed into the stuffy carriage smell. She turned round to face Jessica. Now she looked almost calm.

"You will write? Promise. Write often."

"Of course I will."

"And try to explain for me to Aunt Lydia."

The guard blew his whistle, the train went shunt, shunt, shunt, gathered steam. Jessica put her hand on the carriage window and walked, walked faster, ran. When the carriage slipped away she went on running beside the train as Maimie must have run along the platform in Edinburgh, until it was no longer any good.

Then she stood and waved.

# 18

## *She's Gone*

Jessica had always mistrusted railway stations; but she was not prepared for the terrible depression which settled on her when she stopped running. She stood still for a second, staring after the train, and then walked slowly back to the station entrance.

The High Street was still full of shoppers. They ambled along, whole families, baskets laden and eyes vacant. Jessica dodged in and around them, tough and slippery as a small boy just out of the pictures. Nobody would have guessed how awful she was feeling, that nothing could ever be nice and ordinary again.

It was not until she arrived at the Crescent and at the very gate of her own house that Jessica realized that the house was shut, empty, and that she had no way of getting in. Well, it was all one to her whether she waited for her mother sitting on the front step or in an armchair in the sitting-room. Half-heartedly she wandered round to the back door and tried the handle. Locked, of course. But the window over the kitchen sink had been left open an inch or two at the bottom. The effort of heaving it up, heaving herself on to the high sill, stepping into, and finally over the sink, occupied her for a few minutes so completely that when she finally landed on the floor with a jump, the shock of what had happened rushed back at her again.

The curtains had been closed everywhere against the sun. It looked as if someone was dead. Jessica lagged upstairs and stood in the open doorway of her parents' bedroom. On the dressing-table propped up against the silver-framed photograph of her father was the note. She crossed the silent room and picked it up. "Aunt Lydia" it said, in Isobel's neat hand. Somehow, it was the sight of this folded piece of paper which made Jessica realize exactly why she was feeling so awful. Twenty minutes ago she had been wholly identified with Isabel. Nobody mattered but Isabel and her unhappiness. But now, without being aware of how the change had taken place, it was her family who mattered; *their* feelings. She looked again at the note still in her hand. "Aunt Lydia" . . . Mother: how shocked and hurt she would be. She pictured her mother coming into the room, snatching it up, reading it, felt all her anxiety and bewilderment, her sense of failure. For they had, all of them, somehow failed Isabel. All her mother's kindness and gentleness and tact had ended in this.

Jessica walked slowly into her own bedroom. The sight of Claudius curled round in a cosy nest on her coverlet, one paw draped over his eyes, did lighten her heart for a second. Naughty, darling Claudius, taking advantage, sneaking so pleased through the empty house to her room. She gathered his warmth into her arms and lay with him on the bed. Through the open door came the sound of the grandfather clock in the hall striking four, its notes vibrant in the muted light. So there was a whole hour to wait at the very least before she could expect her family back again. . . .

In the heavily silent house the front door opened. Footsteps filled the hall, voices. . . .

"Jessica! Jessica! Are you in? Where are you?"

Her mother's voice, sharp with anxiety, woke her from a doze. Jessica scrambled off the bed in a panic and appeared at the top of the stairs, red-faced and dishevelled.

"Jessica, just tell me at once what you've been up to. Rosalind said you never helped with the refreshments at all, just disappeared."

They were all staring up at her: Mother, Uncle Richard, Rosalind and Sophie; all focussing their accusing eyes on her. It was a shock to Jessica. She simply had not realized until that moment how her own disappearance might have caused anger and anxiety. On the top of everything else, it was too much. She flung herself down the stairs and at her mother crying, "It's Isabel. She's gone!"

For a moment her mother held her tight as if she realized it was the only thing to do. Then she drew Jessica away from her so that she could look down into her face.

"Jessica, what do you mean? Stop shaking, dear, and try and tell me quietly."

"I couldn't stop her. I met her on the way to the station. She's gone back to Maimie in Edinburgh. She . . . . she didn't like being with *any* of us."

If Jessica had realized, this was her great moment; her moment of identification with her family. But she only heard her own voice with the familiar sense of her inadequacy. Her blunt words had helped neither her mother nor Isabel. . . .

"Lydia, is there anything I can do?" That was Uncle Richard.

"It's five now. If she's catching the five from King's Cross, we're too late to do anything. Except phone through to Edinburgh. Oh, Rick, would you do that? Get through to Mrs. McMillan and explain. Tell her I'll ring later. . . . Now, Jessica. . . ."

It still sounded as if the whole thing was her fault. Jessica pressed her hands over her hot cheeks and burst into tears. . . .

She cried for a moment or two in her mother's arms, and then felt better. By then Uncle Richard had got through to Edinburgh and handed the phone over to his sister.

Her mother was nearly ten minutes talking over the phone to Mrs. McMillan. Then she returned to the sitting-room where everyone was standing about awkwardly.

"Mrs. McMillan says she can't understand it. She quite thought that Isabel had settled down. She's promised to meet Isabel's train and she'll phone back here tomorrow morning after Isabel's arrival. Oh, and she says she'll have a serious talk with Maimie. . . ." She sat down in a chair and looked tired. "Well, I can't think what went wrong. We did all try our best."

"Don't worry, Mum," said Rosalind. "We did everything we possibly could."

This was the moment for Jessica to produce a few tactful explanations. But how could she mention stray cats and "being saddled with her" while Uncle Richard was in the room, or embark on a halting explanation of Isabel's hidden desire to be a nurse, her fierce and equally secret opposition to studying Geography? Perhaps this was one of those times when it was wise and adult to keep quiet.

Then Sophie, the belle of the afternoon, the precious, gifted child, gave one enormous yawn.

Everybody turned their heads in her direction. Sophie looked back at them out of her enormous eyes.

"Sophie, darling, you're tired. . . . Well, we're not doing any good just standing around. We could all do with some coffee and sandwiches, I expect. . . ."

The wheels began to move again. Fifteen minutes later Sophie, in her dressing-gown, was drinking a glass of milk on her mother's knee; Rosalind, unwontedly subdued, was making the coffee in the kitchen; Uncle Richard stared out of the window; Jessica, unbidden for once in her life, laid the table for the evening meal. Then she heard the gate click and saw Mr. Rendell come up the path, the evening paper under his arm, and pause to look at the greenfly on the roses.

"It's Daddy," she said to her mother, with a sense of relief.

Mr. Rendell certainly made everyone feel better.

"You mustn't feel too bad about it, Lydia. Isabel was bound to go through a bad patch before settling down here or anywhere. And there's no doubt she's been working a bit too hard, and on top of that she's had a sharp attack of homesickness. But I'm afraid the poor girl will find herself no nearer the home she wants simply by running back to her Edinburgh."

"She says, we're not her real relations; that we're just saddled with her," burst from Jessica.

"But, Jessica, when she's had time to calm down, she'll realize she hasn't solved her problem by exchanging one roof for another. She'll soon start thinking that the McMillans are saddled with her."

"She means to get a job. I'm sure she does."

"Little girls of fifteen like her can't get jobs. . . . No, she's got to come to terms with her situation, and realize that we do want her, and not just for her mother's sake."

"She didn't like us."

"Oh, fiddle. She was afraid we didn't like her. Under that veneer of pretty manners she's as thin-skinned as you make them. She bottled up her feelings until ——"

The telephone rang. Everybody looked excited and hopeful. Mr. Rendell took a swift step to the door.

"I'll answer it. It may be only someone wanting an appointment."

He returned at once. "Rick, it's for you."

Uncle Richard, surprised, left the room unobtrusively. He was talking for nearly five minutes in the hall, and then returned, equally quietly, to the sitting-room. He sat down in the armchair facing the window, and Claudius came and settled himself along the full length of his knee. Jessica was pleased. Claudius kneaded his claws in and out of Uncle Richard's trouser leg, and Uncle Richard said, "Ouch" very softly and unhooked them. And that was all he did say.

There was no news from Edinburgh that night. But at seven o'clock the next morning, the phone rang in the Rendells' bedroom. Mr. Rendell was sure it was an emergency call, and groaned as he answered it. But no, the faint voice at the other end was Mrs. McMillan's. Isabel had arrived safely late last night.

Everybody was down to breakfast early that Sunday, even Jessica. She plied her mother with questions.

Yes, Isabel had arrived safely. She seemed very tired, very overwrought, and was being kept in bed. Mrs. McMillan was quite sure that she was suffering from delayed shock and that it might do her good to have Maimie to talk to. Mrs. Rendell did not disclose over the breakfast table that she had also had a word with Maimie, but after breakfast she said:

"Jess, you can help me dry up this morning. Rosalind, you run upstairs and take the sheets off Isabel's bed."

Yesterday morning Jessica would have considered that Rosalind had been given the better job of the two. But this morning she had the feeling that her mother had something for her ears alone. She picked up the drying-up cloth and stood, quiet and receptive, at her mother's side.

"Jess, I had a few words with Maimie on the phone. She wanted to speak to me. She said, amongst other things, that Isabel sent you her love."

"Oh . . ."

"I didn't realize, Jess, that Isabel was so fond of you."

Jessica dried a cup very carefully. "I knew she found Rosalind a bit too much. But I thought she despised me."

Her mother said nothing. Jessica realized that the situation was a delicate one. Rosalind, stripping a bed upstairs, would not know she had been intentionally sent out of ear-shot; she was so quick, she'd be with them again in a minute. And was she, even now, no longer busily engaged upstairs? A clear, familiar voice could be heard talking over the phone in the hall.

"Yes, she just cleared off . . . like that. . . . Well, Clare, I did have to be nice to her; you do see that. . . . Yes, come round to tea. You may find us all a bit piano. . . . Oh, rubbish, you won't be intruding on our grief. . . . Oh, all right, then. See you Monday. 'Bye. . . ."

Mrs. Rendell and Jessica exchanged glances. It was a nice moment for Jessica. She could almost feel herself growing more mature; the recipient of adult confidences.

But it was not a very cheerful Sunday. Even Rosalind, bright though she had sounded over the phone, was not her usual bubbling self. Nobody could shake off for long the thought that Isabel had been unhappy with them; and was, no doubt, feeling just as unhappy now. Jessica knew in her heart that however much relief Isabel would get from talking and talking and talking to her old friend Maimie she was far too sensitive not to realize more and more acutely all the grief and pain and anxiety she must have caused. After all, even if there were no bonds of blood between Isabel and her Aunt Lydia, there were other bonds. She couldn't just clear off and feel nothing. Poor Isabel.

So Sunday passed slowly and heavily. And it was not until she went to bed that night that Jessica's mind turned to school. Her heart sank. She had forgotten all about school and its problems. But there waiting for her was the problem of Nance and her Awful Suggestion.

Tomorrow she *must* tackle Mr. Stephens about Uncle Richard, look Nance in the face again. It seemed a pity to come through Saturday's fiery ordeals feeling older and wiser; and then feel unable to tackle Monday's. . . .

# 19

# *Everything Comes Right After All*

Rosalind came down to breakfast on Monday morning looking as fresh as a rose. The first thing she said was:

"Mum, what am I to say at school about Isabel? Does Miss Elliott know she's run away?"

"There's no need for you to say anything at all, except that Isabel is unwell. I rang Miss Elliott last night and I've an appointment to see her this morning."

"But what will you say to her? Suppose Isabel comes back to us? Suppose she *doesn't* come back? Miss Elliott will want everything very cut and dried."

"I shall know what to say, Rosalind."

Jessica cast a glance of respect at her mother. Trying though it was to have an ex-teacher from a famous school for a mother, she could not help feeling pleased that her mother was more than able to cope with the august Miss Elliott.

"Rick," said her mother—she had turned to Uncle Richard—"I could only get an appointment for eleven—if you would switch on the oven for me at eleven-thirty. . . ."

Uncle Richard looked startled.

"I'm awfully sorry, Lydia, but I've got an appointment at eleven too."

"Oh, Rick, about a job? How splendid. Where?"

"I don't exactly know *where* yet. But I've got an appointment with Mr. Stephens. Jessica ——" and here Uncle Richard broke off and grinned at Jessica—"seems to have been doing a bit of homework for me."

The cup of coffee which had been half-way to Jessica's lips remained there. It moved neither up nor down.

"Rick, what on earth are you talking about? And what has Jessica been doing?"

"Nothing, Mother," said Jessica quickly. Her head was spinning.

But Uncle Richard continued to grin at Jessica.

"Apparently, she's boosted me up as a first-class lecturer on Wild Life in Africa. So he wants to fix a date with me. But he also says that he knows someone at the Zoo . . ."

If there had been lines of strain on her mother's face since Saturday evening, Jessica saw them vanish now.

"Oh, Rick, I'm so terribly pleased. But how long have you known about this? Why didn't you tell us before?"

"You remember that phone call on Saturday night? That was Jessica's head-master."

"But you shouldn't have kept such splendid news to yourself even for a minute."

"There are times for everything," said Uncle Richard. And he gave a quick wink at Jessica.

"Jessica, I'd love to know exactly what part you've played in this," said Mrs. Rendell.

"I'd like to know myself," said Jessica. "I only got as far as telling Mr. Berryman."

Mr. Rendell got up and flicked Jessica's head with his newspaper.

"Good for you, Jess."

"Uncle Richard," said Jessica. She blotted everyone else out, spoke only to her uncle. "It was really Nance, not me."

"I'm very much obliged to you *both*," said Uncle Richard.

Jessica suddenly felt very happy. When Uncle Richard said "both" like that, all the awkwardness between herself and Nance seemed to melt away. True, she had failed to do the one thing which Nance had wanted her to do; but, somehow, miraculously, the "awful idea" had succeeded without it. And Nance must be told as soon as possible. It was Nance who was the heroine of the hour.

"Mum, need I clear the breakfast things this morning? I want to call round at Nance's house before Bunny has a chance of catching me."

"I'll do Jessica's chores," said Uncle Richard quickly. He had forgotten about Sophie.

"Run along, Jess," said her mother.

Jessica ran.

The hanging basket over the porch had just been watered and dripped down on to Jessica's nose. The tiles shone red with Cardinal polish. Jessica pressed the musical bell, and almost at once Nance herself flung the door open, an apron round her middle, as if she did chores before school too.

"Jess!" She staggered back, theatrically stunned; and then grinned all over her face.

"I thought I'd call round for you."

"Give me two secs."

Nance jerked off her apron, snatched her beret from a little peg in the tiny hall, snatched her satchel from another, bawled out, " 'Bye, Ma. Jess has called round for me," stepped briskly over the step and banged the door behind them.

"Nance," said Jessica earnestly, "Uncle is awfully obliged to you."

"Obliged to me?" cried Nance.

And then out came the story. Out came *both* stories: for however pleased and happy Jessica felt about her uncle, the thought of Isabel, far away in Edinburgh, was never far from her mind. She talked the whole way to school without stopping, talked in the cloakroom, talked along the corridor and in at the classroom door, and would have gone on with her tale if she hadn't found Mr. Berryman in the class-room before her.

"Ah, Jessica!" he said, as she came in at the door.

Jessica went dumb and advanced to his side.

"I expect that Mr. Stephens has already been in touch with your uncle . . ." he waited for Jessica's nod; and then went on. "I turned up to watch a cricket match here on Saturday, and some of our boys began telling me about your uncle. I did wonder how you'd got on with Mr. Stephens so I mentioned you and your uncle to him. He said . . . well, Jessica, what he actually said was that you'd evidently taken fright at the last moment . . ."

Jessica stared back at Mr. Berryman, shamed, hypnotized.

"Well, never mind; I was able to do the telling for you."

"Oh, thank you, Mr. Berryman. Thank you awfully."

"A pleasure, Jessica."

Mr. Berryman *was* a nice man. Jessica realized with dismay that next term she would have a different form-master. Kind, clumsy, breezy Mr. Berryman, who understood her so well, would be exchanged for someone who wasn't so quick in the uptake.

Anyhow, she could still feel happy and relieved about Uncle Richard. The guilt of the postal order was blotted out. Perhaps never again would she have to watch Uncle Richard jingling coppers in his pocket while he stared, hopeless and bored to death, out of their window.

If only she could feel equally happy about Isabel.

The end of the summer term was only two weeks off. In the meantime letters passed between Mrs. McMillan and Mrs. Rendell; between Mrs. Rendell and Isabel's former head-mistress in Edinburgh; between Mrs. McMillan and Miss Elliott. Rosalind and Jessica were both wild with curiosity but all their mother would say was, "We must wait and see." Uncle Richard gave a talk on "Wild Life in Africa" and was a roaring success; then he gave another talk to the Boys' Grammar School out at Wedgetree, and came home looking brisk and happy. The next day he packed a small suitcase and went up to Scotland for an interview.

The day after that came a letter from Isabel to her Aunt Lydia. She had asked to come back.

For the past fortnight Rosalind and Jessica had been unbearably tantalized by the way in which their mother had read through long letters with the Edinburgh postmark and then put them back again into their envelopes without a single remark.

But this morning was different.

"Come back *now*?" asked Rosalind.

"No; the McMillans are going to Austria for their holiday and want to take Isabel with them. She'll come back here a day or two before the Autumn term begins. She will be moved up, of course, but into a different stream. Miss Elliott says there are quite half-a-dozen girls who are thinking of taking up nursing, and they are all to be together in the 'B' stream. She'll still have plenty of opportunity for her Geography, of course, but a lot of emphasis will be given to the subjects that will be most use to her if she wants to enter a good London hospital."

Rosalind spoke without her usual impulsiveness.

"So . . . if I move up with the 'A' stream . . . we shan't be together?"

"Darling, you *are* going up with the 'A' stream, so you won't be together."

Jessica regarded Rosalind from under her fringe. Her sister seemed to be thinking a lot before she spoke.

"We'll hardly ever see each other once we're in school . . . and our homework will be different. Of course, I can still help her with her Latin. . . ."

"Rosalind . . ." now it was her mother who seemed to be hesitating—"I don't think that is going to hurt either of you. You helped her to find her feet and now . . . well, I think that stage is past, and she will want to make her own friends. You see, you and Isabel didn't choose each other. Clare was your choice, and you have been neglecting her."

"Jessica and I didn't choose each other. But we get on."

"Do we?" cried Jessica, in sceptical tones.

"Hush, Jessica. . . . Rosalind, you and Jessica are sisters, but Isabel is not even a real cousin. You must let her give her affection where she likes."

The letters that arrived for Jessica from Scotland, and later from Austria, made that matter quite clear to everyone.

* * *

The *real* summer holiday was over. The McMillans had come back from Austria, Rosalind had come back with her school from a holiday in Luxemburg, Mr. and Mrs. Rendell and Jessica and Sophie had come back from Suffolk; Claudius had been collected from a holiday home for cats. And Uncle Richard?

Uncle Richard was busy packing his big suitcase. He had been away on a six weeks' refresher course, and was now off to Scotland to take up a post in the new Zoological Gardens. Rosalind worked out, after doing an Algebraic calculation, that if Uncle Richard looked out of his train window about 9.30 at night he might catch a glimpse of Isabel through her train window as she went rushing south.

Jessica hugged her uncle goodbye. It was a pity she couldn't have both of them: Uncle Richard and Isabel; but it was better this way. As soon as he had been given his big send-off Mrs. Rudge would bustle in with her hoover and polish and dusters. Isabel would have a room of her own again.

The house seemed very quiet after Uncle Richard had

gone. Strange, when he had made so little noise. Jessica went up to her bedroom feeling quite beside herself with depression, and found on her chest-of-drawers two parcels. One, which looked like a box of chocolates, was addressed to "Miss Nance O'Neill"; the other had "Jess, with love from her God-father" written on it.

It was a biggish, shapeless parcel, and it contained ten tubes of oil paints, three brushes and a bottle of turpentine.

The smell, Jessica thought, was *heavenly*.

Isabel was to arrive, as she had arrived that Sunday three months ago, soon after breakfast. There had been no argument as to who should meet her at the station. Rosalind had accepted the fact without any show of surprise when Jessica and her mother drove off alone in the car.

"Jessica," said her mother, when they reached the station approach, "I'll wait here. Get your platform ticket and go on to Platform number 6. Isabel will feel better if it's only you."

Jessica did as she was told. She bought her ticket, climbed the stairs, stood on the grey platform. She was scared. Anybody would think she was Isabel's aunt. Yet, somehow, she accepted the challenge. She braced her legs, clutched her ticket and stared up the empty track.

It was ages before a voice called through a loud speaker, "The train from London is now approaching platform 6." Another age before the signal fell. Another age before the train, tiny, was suddenly there, way down the track, swelling larger, larger.

Jessica took a nervous step nearer the edge of the platform, cleared her throat. The next few moments were all confusion. The monster engine roared towards her, roared past, stopped; windows crashed down, doors opened, people spilled out. Jessica ran this way and that, bumping into people.

Then she saw Isabel. Head bent, she was struggling with her luggage.

Jessica raised her hand and seized the handle. They heaved together. It reached the platform with a thud.

Then Isabel jumped out after it. And the first words she said were: "Oh, Jess, I'm glad it's you."